Practical Astrology and Planetary Magick

An Essential Guide to Astrological Transits, Reading Natal Charts, Magickal Spells, and More

Your Free Gift
(only available for a limited time)

Thanks for getting this book! If you want to learn more about various spirituality topics, then join Mari Silva's community and get a free guided meditation MP3 for awakening your third eye. This guided meditation mp3 is designed to open and strengthen ones third eye so you can experience a higher state of consciousness. Simply visit the link below the image to get started.

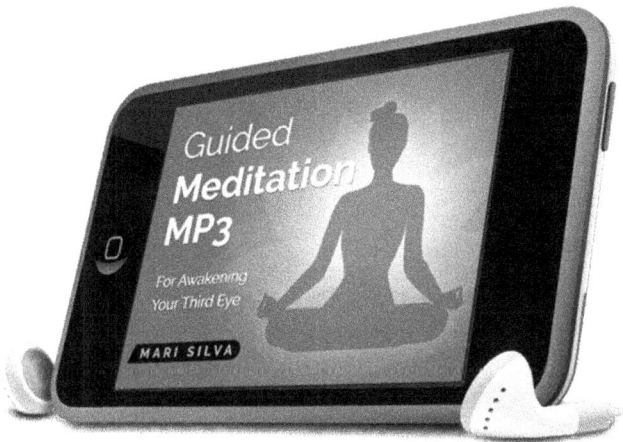

https://spiritualityspot.com/meditation

Table of Contents

Part 1: Practical Astrology

The Ultimate Guide to Astrological Transits, Predictive Astrology, Reading Natal Charts, and More

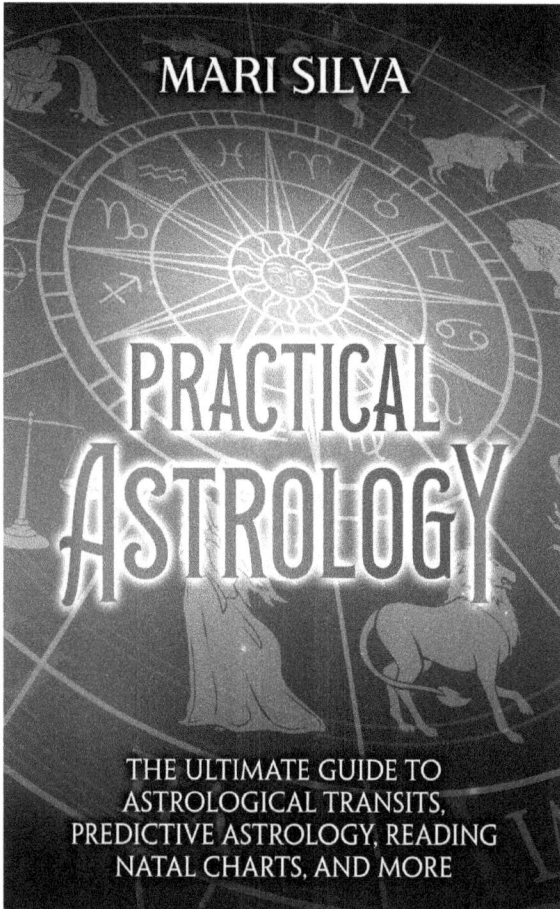

Introduction

Astrology has been around for a long time and is both older and more complex than most people in the West realize. Going back to the ancient cultures of Mesopotamia, Greece, and other locales of early human civilization, astrology has emerged with several applications, purposes, methods, and areas of focus. People have long looked to astrology for self-reflection, insight into other people's natures and personalities, relationships, and perhaps even insight into what the future might hold in store.

Indeed, while aspects of astrology have been associated with practices like divination, worship, and religious dogma – particularly in the old days – most folks tend to see astrology as something that has a place in daily life in a very practical sense. This is especially true nowadays, and, as you'll see in this book, astrology is something that anyone can get into quite easily and reach a significant level of proficiency.

This book's goal is to teach you everything you need to know, not just to start studying astrology but also to apply it in your life and make the most out of it. Our focus will be on practical astrology, but to learn how to engage in this practice properly, you'll also learn much about the inner workings of this ancient discipline. Astrology also happens to be a rather popular topic nowadays, especially in the West, so there is no shortage of literature on the subject. However, many astrology books are rather complicated, convoluted, and don't really do a good job helping novices get into practical astrology in a concise, comprehensive, and highly understandable manner. The hands-on instructions will also ensure a high degree of practical applicability once you've absorbed everything we'll explore in the ensuing chapters.

As you've probably noticed, even though everyone knows about astrology, most people's engagement with it doesn't go past reading the daily horoscope during their lunch break. If you want to go past this level and see what practical astrology offers on a deeper level, you'll find that this book is precisely the guide you need. By exploring the intricacies of how astrology works and influences us and how things like natal charts work, you'll realize that there is a whole world out there to learn about beyond the surface.

You might be surprised to realize how much influence the planets have on you. By the time you conclude this book, you'll find many overlaps between your experiences and what the stars are telling you. More importantly, you'll likely learn new things about yourself and your life. These realizations can open up some interesting new paths you may not have been aware of before.

Chapter 1: Introduction to Practical Astrology

As briefly mentioned, astrology is an ancient tool that humanity has used for millennia. No practice or philosophy can endure that long and even become more popular with time without it bringing quite a few interesting things to the table. Across generations, cultures, nations, religions, and civilizations, people have used astrology to peer into their future and, most importantly, into themselves. Over time, astrology has evolved and changed quite a bit, both in complexity and in how it's applied in practice. Astrology has also adapted to different cultures and their particular interests, contributing to the development of the practice as a whole.

Much of what we talk about in this book will be through the lens of Western astrology, which will be the main focus. Before we get into the details of how Western astrology works nowadays, we'll use an introductory chapter to explore the earliest recorded use of astrology and how it gradually developed to the point where it is today. We'll also lay down some of the basics of practical astrology, giving you a solid foundational understanding of everything else we'll cover in the coming chapters.

The History of Astrology and Its Spread in the West

There was a time when the history of astrology was, in a way, also the history of astronomy. Back in ancient times, people observed the celestial bodies in the skies and tried to learn as much about them as possible, giving rise to all the stories told along the way. At the same time, ancient folks wondered how those planets and stars affected them and their lives. It took a while for astronomy and astrology to diverge into clearly distinct disciplines, with the former taking on a strictly scientific shape. At the same time, the latter focused on the spiritual, emotional, and intangible.

It all likely began in ancient Mesopotamia around 3000 BC or earlier when people first started to wonder about the stars above. Early civilizations like the Sumerians had a distinct fascination with the celestial arrangements they saw. Around 3000 BC, they began identifying, naming, and recording what they saw. Even before that, the Sumerians made rock paintings and other depictions of planets and their movements, especially the sun and the moon, which they saw as having a great effect on our world. These depictions have been discovered to go as far back as 5000 BC.

These folks were quick to take note of prominent constellations thanks to the keen ability of the human mind to notice patterns. The Babylonians made considerable early contributions in terms of isolating and naming various constellations and celestial bodies. This civilization began to flourish after the 18th century BC and was responsible for introducing an early form of the zodiac. This was simply based on the sequence of constellations across the sky above. The Babylonians observed the planets of our solar system as they moved in front of these constellations or across their path.

The Babylonians eventually divided the zodiac into twelve equal zones based on twelve easily discernable constellations. They named many of these constellations after animals and other things from daily life and culture. These concepts eventually spread and reached ancient Greece to the northwest, where the system was named *zodiakos kyklos*, meaning the "animal circle." These were the beginnings of astrology in Europe and, subsequently, the Western world.

Astrology probably began to take on its familiar form when people first began noticing that certain celestial positions and events tended to correlate with events on our planet. Ancient Babylonians would construct so-called star towers, which they used solely to observe the visible universe to get a better look. Some of the earliest notes they made about the sky included the fact that some stars and planets seemed to stay put while others moved across the sky. This very rudimentary, early observation soon paved the way for more realizations, and it wasn't long until an entire discipline evolved around the observation of the heavens.

The ancients initially associated things like planetary movements and alignments with earthly events that they deemed important, such as the crowning of kings. It wasn't long until folks began to give all sorts of religious associations and connotations to the stars above, and that's when both astronomy and astrology really took off. Apart from ancient Mesopotamian cultures like the Sumerians and Akkadians (Babylonians), ancient Egyptians also included the stars in their worship.

Egypt was most likely the source from which astrology made its way to ancient Greece. It's difficult to say with absolute certainty, but one theory is that Persia adopted certain traditions after their conquests of Egypt before being conquered by Alexander the Great. All three of these cultures had some form of astrological practice. Still, Alexander's conquests led to a fusion of these traditions and subsequently the emergence of Hellenistic astrology, also known as traditional astrology. This is one of the ancient schools of astrology that persists to this day. From then on, ancient Greeks developed astrology and its disciplines quite a lot while also making advancements in astronomy.

This fusion of traditions occurred during the 3rd and 2nd centuries BC in Alexandria in what was then Hellenic Egypt under the Ptolemaic dynasty, established by Alexander the Great during his conquests. Scholars in Alexandria were the ones who adopted Babylonian astrology from Mesopotamia and combined it with pre-Hellenic astrological traditions of Egypt. This was how the concept of Horoscopic astrology as we know it today emerged. The Babylonian traditions contributed to the idea of the zodiac wheel and planetary exaltations, among other elements. The zodiac was then divided into 36 parts of ten degrees according to Egyptian ideas, which were implemented in a way that revolved around Greek gods and their corresponding planets and the elements and sign rulership.

Some of the most important developments in this early Western astrology are owed to the Greek and Roman astrologer and astronomer called Ptolemy. Ptolemy lived between 100 and 170 AD in Alexandria during Roman times in Egypt. One of his central contributions to horoscopic astrology was the Tetrabiblos ("Four Books"). These writings provided the foundations of Western astrology's further development and would become legendary among astrologers for the next two millennia. The text was subsequently translated into Latin in the 12th century and would continue to circulate throughout Medieval Europe from that point on, which helped spread its influence far and wide.

Before Europe's interest in astrology was rekindled, astrology made significant headway in the Arab world during the Dark Ages in Europe, since its teachings were frowned upon by established Christian dogma. Arabs also spread the practice during their expansions during the 7th and 8th centuries across Asia, the Middle East, and North Africa. Beyond just horoscopic astrology, the Arabs during that time preserved a strong interest in astronomy and the discoveries of Ptolemy, building observatories and developing devices such as the astrolabe. They held astrology in high regard as a means of predicting the future and a source of guidance in life in general.

The true resurgence of astrology in Europe came during the Renaissance. By the late Renaissance in the 17th century, Western astrology had come a long way and had become quite complex. For at least three millennia up to that point, astrology had evolved into a practice enriched by numerous great cultures, making it a unique fusion that lay somewhere between science and divinity. Throughout the Renaissance, astrology was a practice accomplished scientists, intellectuals, and philosophers often engaged in as a side project. This was how astrology made its way into universities, art, literature, and even architecture, permeating all facets of the Western world.

Astrology entered a period of decline from the late 17th century onward. It's difficult to say what caused this decline. Still, it was likely a mixture of factors ranging from a sharp turn toward rigid, hard science to intolerance by the religious establishment, particularly in the Catholic world. There are no records of astrologers being persecuted by religious authorities in the West. Still, the growing skepticism of the Catholic Church toward the practice most likely contributed to a sharp decline in popularity and favor for astrology in the political and social arenas.

The advent of the modern scientific method and the Newtonian principles in science likely dealt the final blow to astrology as an established practice in all layers of society. Before the 17th century, astrology was being practiced even in the judicial system, but that slowly changed, starting in the 17th century. In the latter half of the 18th century, astrology was banished from universities, cutting the practice off from Western intellectual circles. Apart from pushing astrology into more obscure waters, these changes affected the quality of the practice. As time went on, fewer intellectuals and scientists engaged in the practice, reducing the rate at which the discipline developed.

Nonetheless, astrology persevered as a practice and as an object of much fascination over the next couple of centuries until seeing a significant resurgence in the 20th century. One may even argue that astrology is now more widely popularized than it's ever been in the past few thousand years. In fact, astrology has even started to slowly creep its way back into intellectual circles, with a growing number of academics showing an interest.

The Basics of Practical Astrology

Even though many strictly scientific minds consider astrology a pseudoscience, it has repeatedly shown itself to have been beneficial. After all, it's not surprising that scientists don't look too kindly on astrology, but this doesn't take away from the practice since astrology never did strive to compete with science in the first place. It has no ambition or reason to compete with physics or chemistry but instead seeks to venture beyond the usual thinking box to find answers that science simply isn't equipped to answer.

Over the years, some scientists have tried to set up some sort of scientific basis or model for astrology, although with limited progress. For example, a French psychologist and statistician named Michel Gauquelin has researched some interesting astrological correlations. Namely, he found that statistically speaking, there are indicative connections and planetary placements in the birth charts of successful people in sports, arts, and many other arenas.

The pursuit of scientific answers regarding astrology may or may not produce results in the long run, but the practice continues to grow in popularity regardless of the outcome of such pursuits. Astrology has become so popular that it's entered the daily lives of millions or even billions of people worldwide, which is precisely where astrology is most at home. The practice has blossomed into that which it has always strived to be. This is a tool regular and distinguished people like to try to find themselves and their purpose in this universe while learning how to become better people.

When you get down to it, that's really what astrology is! It's a guide that provides people with insights they can't get anywhere else, which can do virtually no harm and only provide you with opportunities to make positive changes and get ahead. At the very least, it's about learning to empathize more with yourself and with other people through learning and understanding.

Even though it isn't an exact study, astrology is best defined in practical terms as a field of study that focuses on a subtle, causal connection between what happens with the celestial bodies above us and the events that happen on our planet. Those invested in this field of study and practicing its methods are known as astrologers. Practical astrology generally focuses on areas most people are interested in, such as careers, health in the broadest sense, relationships, general luck or fortune, and other similar areas of human life.

Weekly and monthly horoscopes are the most common manifestations of astrology in daily life, but astrology goes infinitely deeper than the entertainment section of a daily or weekly magazine. As you'll find out in this book, astrology is a complex practice with many layers and a lot to unpack on the theoretical side of things. Because of this, professional astrologers are dedicated, well-versed, and informed experts who use extensive theoretical knowledge to read the celestial events that go on around us and their implications on our lives.

One of the most central matters that practical astrology focuses on is the position of the sun, moon, and planets of the solar system at the moment of your birth. As you'll learn in this book, the placements of these celestial bodies in the sky are a key theme and the source of most astrologers' predictions and analyses. On top of that, the movement of those objects is another key factor that plays a part in your astrological destiny, with a particular focus on forecasts. To that end, practical astrology focuses on two main areas in terms of the things it can teach you; analysis of your personality and forecasts about your future.

Practical astrology studies the inherent traits and energies of the planets that make up our solar system, plus the moon and the sun. More advanced astrology also considers many other celestial bodies that can be found wandering around our system. Through the ensuing chapters, we'll take a closer look at the characteristics of all these objects and how they interact with you. Of course, another major area of focus covers the twelve zodiac signs we're all familiar with. These signs have inherent traits and characteristics that make them unique and cause them to interact with the planets in certain ways. Beyond the signs and the planets, practical astrology studies many other factors, such as planetary aspects, progressions, astrological houses, and much more. These are the fundamentals that every aspiring astrologer must first grasp before moving on to doing their own astrological readings with competence.

The phrase *"As above, so below"* is perhaps the best summary of astrology. This phrase has likely been around for centuries or even millennia and has been associated with religion and various other parts of the human experience. However, in astrology, it's a literal, word-for-word description. "As the universe, so the soul" often follows the first phrase, communicating astrology's message that our lives, experiences, potential, purpose, love, pain, and soul are constantly influenced by something much greater; something that goes on above us as we sleep, walk, and talk and will continue for eternity long after we are gone.

Chapter 2: The Planets

Solar system.
https://pixabay.com/images/id-3880590/

Since the very essence of astrology is how celestial bodies and their properties influence you and your life, the most important initial step toward mastering practical astrology is to learn more about the planets, particularly their energy. Even though the nine planets, the moon, and the sun of our solar system are generally the strongest influences, there are many other celestial bodies to consider, as you'll learn later in the book. For now, we will focus primarily on the nine planets of our solar system, as well as the sun and the moon, both of which are classified as planets in astrology and are also known as "luminaries" in astrology because they are the brightest objects in the sky.

Sun

- **Color:** Gold
- **Stones:** Tiger's eye, citrine, carnelian, ruby
- **Keywords:** Ego, personality, vitality, consciousness

Just like zodiac signs, all planets have their individual glyphs, which are symbols that represent them and their characteristics in a brief, concise, and visual manner. The sun's glyph is a simple circle with a dot in the middle, representing life and the sun's central role in everything that has to do with life, personally and in general.

Astrologers often refer to the sun as the luminary of life, the self, or the ego. Like other planets, the sun has certain keywords that best describe what the planet symbolizes, including personality, consciousness, vitality, confidence, and creativity. The sun also possesses distinctly masculine energy, often ruling the male influences in your life. The sun takes about a month to transit between zodiac signs and twelve months to go through the entire zodiac.

The sun is exalted when in Aries, in fall when in Libra, and in detriment in Aquarius. Like all other planets and important celestial bodies, the sun has had many divine associations across different cultures throughout history. It has been associated with the Roman sun god Sol Invictus, the Greek Apollo and Helios, and Babylonian Shamash. The sun's energy is the essence of everyone's self and determines who we are and how we express that to the world. Its immense power is evident in most Leos, which is the sign that the sun rules.

Moon

- **Color:** Silver
- **Stones:** Moonstone, Celestine, amethyst
- **Keywords:** Subconscious, instinct, habits, emotions, mood

The moon is represented by a crescent, a self-explanatory glyph. Still, it also has some more subtle meanings, representing our emotional side, evolution, and the hidden nature of things. Thus, astrologers generally refer to the moon as the luminary of emotions, associating it with instincts, habits, the subconscious, memories, intuition, mood, and other subtle characteristics that make you who you are.

The moon quickly transitions between zodiac signs, taking only two to three days. Furthermore, the luminary of emotions is exalted in Taurus, in detriment in Capricorn, and in fall when in Scorpio. Traditionally, it has been associated with the Roman deities such as Luna and Diana, Greek Selene and Artemis, Babylonian Sin, and others. Simply put, the moon is all about your inner world and has tremendous influence over your mood and the mood of all humanity. In many ways, the subtle and serene nature of the moon's energy is the opposite of the sun. Whereas the sun rules how you express yourself and relate to the outside world, the moon is a reflective force that guides self-reflection and self-discovery. This luminary rules Cancer, a sign that exhibits many of the moon's traits.

Mercury

- **Color:** Orange

- **Stones:** Fluorite, onyx, aquamarine

- **Keywords:** Communication, reason, intelligence, language, mind

Mercury's glyph, also called Mercury's caduceus, consists of one central circle with a cross dangling from its bottom and a half-circle protruding from its top, resembling two horns. The cross was a 16th-century addition and is interpreted by some astrologers as a representation of the true, inner self that longs to be expressed and manifested. The horns on the top of the glyph make the symbol stand out, signifying an inclination toward something higher, particularly in terms of understanding and intellect.

Mercury takes three to four weeks to transition between signs and will be in retrograde four times in 2022, with each retrograde cycle lasting a few weeks. The retrogrades will occur between January 14 and February 3, May 10 and June 3, September 10 and October 2, and December 29 to January 18, 2023.

This planet has traditionally been associated with the Greek god Hermes, the protector of travelers, merchants, and speakers. Similarly, the Babylonians worshiped Mercury as Nabu, representing the god of literacy and wisdom while serving as the protector of scribes. Mercury is in detriment in Sagittarius and Pisces, exalted in Virgo, and in fall when in Pisces. The Romans considered Mercury the messenger of the gods, further illustrating the planet's strong association with communication. This planet's energy is intellectual and curious, influencing our capacity for curiosity, reason, and analysis. Mercury is one of the driving forces behind our desire to express ourselves through all mediums.

Venus

- **Color:** Pink
- **Stones:** Opal, jade, rose quartz
- **Keywords:** Harmony, art, relationships, beauty, love

Venus is represented by a glyph, essentially Mercury's glyph without the half-circle or horns on top. As such, this is the same symbol used to represent the female gender and femininity in general. This is in line with what the planet and its divine equivalents, such as the Roman goddess Venus, have always represented. Venus is a common symbol of female energies, but in a narrower sense in astrology, it represents romance, love, beauty, sexuality, and similar qualities. Venus has also been associated with the Greek deity Aphrodite, worshiped as the goddess of fertility, beauty, passion, and other concepts similar to Venus. The goddess Inanna was the ancient Mesopotamian equivalent of these deities, also associated with Venus.

The transition of Venus between zodiac signs takes around four to five weeks, and the planet has had one retrograde in 2022, lasting between December 19, 2021, and January 29, 2022. Furthermore, Venus finds itself exalted in Pisces, detriment in Aries and Scorpio, and falling in Virgo. Venus's astrological energy and influence are things of beauty, and this planet is generally regarded as one of the most desirable influences in our skies. Venus tends to have tremendous influence over aspects of our lives, with romance, relationships, and attraction, all of which it governs. The loving and beautifying influence of Venus is what brings harmony and joy into life, all while bolstering our creative drive.

Mars

- **Color:** Red
- **Stones:** Bloodstone, garnet, red jasper, carnelian, hematite
- **Keywords:** Passion, courage, aggression, desire, competitiveness

The glyph representing Mars is a circle with an arrow that protrudes and points to the upper right, the same sign used to symbolize the male gender. This is no accident, as many of Mars' traits are associated with masculine energy. In ancient Rome, Mars was worshiped as the god of war, and the planet was associated with similar themes in ancient Greece as the god Ares. Throughout ancient Mesopotamia, Mars was symbolized by Nergal, who also had a connection to war, death, and similar themes.

Mars takes between six and seven weeks to go between zodiac signs, and it's scheduled to go through one retrograde cycle this year, starting on October 30 and ending on January 12, 2023. Mars is exalted in Capricorn, in detriment when in Taurus or Libra, and falls in Cancer. Given the headstrong, aggressive, and highly dynamic nature of Mars and its energy, this is hardly surprising. Mars's aggressive energy is loud and clearly visible for all to see, so it's often considered the warrior among the planets. This planet governs all those fiery influences that drive aggressive and bold individuals, which reflects in Mars' ruled signs of Aries and Scorpio. The energy of Mars is also a physical one, and the planet's position at the time of your birth can influence many physical aspects of your life, such as vitality and athleticism.

Jupiter

- **Color**: Green
- **Stones:** Lapis lazuli, amethyst, topaz, turquoise
- **Keywords:** Growth, expanse, luck, understanding, abundance

Jupiter's glyph consists of a half-circle or crescent with a sideways cross attached on the right side, with the whole symbol resembling a somewhat warped, handwritten number four. Astrologers usually interpret the glyph as having to do with things like learning, deeper understanding, and the evolution that comes with such growth. Just as the cross supports the half-circle, so does Jupiter support, teach, and mentor other gods.

Traditionally, Jupiter has been a helper who would assist other gods in war and all their other endeavors. In Hinduism, for instance, Jupiter has been associated with Guru ("teacher"), also known as Brihaspati ("lord of prayer"), who is an ancient divine figure seen as a sort of counselor of the gods. Jupiter has also played a central role in the pantheons of other ancient cultures. In Greece, it was associated with Zeus, the king of the gods of Olympus. Jupiter, also known as Jove, played a very similar role in ancient Rome.

Jupiter takes a considerable time to transition between signs, usually over a year. It's also scheduled to go through one retrograde cycle in 2022 between July 28 and November 23. This planet is in detriment when in

Gemini or Virgo, exalted in Cancer, and in fall in Capricorn. Jupiter's energy and influence are as massive as this gas giant's physical size. It governs many important aspects of human life, including luck, abundance, wisdom, and spirituality in general. Astrologers also consider Jupiter's energy to be expansive energy, which is why it's the driving force behind the human drive to grow and expand our horizons. Sagittarius particularly exemplifies this.

Saturn

- **Color:** Grey
- **Stones:** Onyx, jet, hematite, tiger's eye
- **Keywords:** Structure, limits, discipline, responsibility, ambition, law, order

Saturn is symbolized by a glyph consisting of an ear-shaped curve with a cross attached to its upper left side. It's a symbol open to some interpretation, with some astrologers suggesting it represents a sort of balance between understanding life and coming to terms with some of the harder facts of existence, including death, aging, and decay. It's also possible that the curve represents a sickle, which would align with Saturn's ancient associations with agriculture. In Greece, for instance, Saturn was known as Cronus, the first of the Titans known for eating his sons due to a prophecy that one would overthrow him as his father did. Cronus was often illustrated as wielding a sickle. As with many other deities and myths, the association carried over into ancient Rome, where Saturn was worshiped as the god of time, generation, dissolution, wealth, and other concepts in addition to agriculture.

Saturn takes longer to transition between signs even further away from the sun than any previously mentioned planet. The transition takes between two and three years. Saturn will also undergo one retrograde between June 4 and October 23 in 2022. Saturn finds itself exalted when it's on Libra, in detriment when in Cancer or Leo, and in fall when it enters Aries. Apart from the associations mentioned above, Saturn is also involved with limits and rules, fostering a sense of discipline. This planet's energy isn't as warm and nurturing as that of some other planets, but it's an influence we need as a species. In ancient Rome, people believed Saturn was the fountainhead of civilization itself because of its ability to bring order.

Uranus

- **Color:** Blue-green
- **Stones:** Aventurine
- **Keywords:** Eccentric, changeable, unpredictable, rebellion

Like Neptune and Pluto, Uranus was discovered relatively recently, so its symbols were first devised in the 18th century. Two glyphs are generally used, with the first being a combination of the alchemical symbols of iron and gold, representing platinum. It's essentially the male symbol with a dot in the middle of the circle and the arrow pointing straight up. The second glyph, more frequently used in astrology, is the Herschel monogram, named after the astronomer who discovered the planet. It consists of a shape very similar to the capital letter "H" and a vertical line that slashes through the middle with a small circle attached at the bottom.

Uranus bears the same name as a Greek deity, who was regarded as the father of the Titans. One such titan is Saturn, husband to Gaia and essentially the god of the sky. This distant planet takes a full seven years to transition between zodiac signs and is experiencing two retrogrades in 2022. The first retrograde began on August 19, 2021, and ended on January 18, 2022, while the second one will start on August 24 and end on January 23, 2023. Uranus is exalted in Scorpio, in detriment in Leo, and in fall in Taurus. The energy of Uranus is a rebellious force, but it also drives innovation, progress, and change in general. Being the first planet discovered with a telescope, Uranus is something of a pioneer among planets.

Neptune

- **Color:** Blue
- **Stones:** Sodalite
- **Keywords:** Intuition, imagination, mysticism, dreams

Being named after the Roman god of the seas Neptune, the equivalent of Greek Poseidon, this planet's glyph is a fairly clear symbol. This symbol is Neptune's trident, a well-known glyph resembling a three-pronged, fork-like shape. Neptune has had an association with water, in general, across different cultures, going beyond just the governance over the seas. For instance, in Indian mythology and Hindu traditions, the equivalent of Neptune is Varuna, the god of rain, sky, justice, truth, and much else.

Neptune takes up to twelve years to transition between signs because of its distance from the sun. It's also scheduled for one retrograde this year, lasting between June 28 and December 4. This planet is exalted in Leo, in detriment in Virgo, and falls in Capricorn. Above all, Neptune's energy is one of mystery and uncertainty. The planet's associations have a lot to do with many of the things that come from deep within us, including dreams. Its energy is also often responsible for illusions, confusion, and all that we find difficult to comprehend. At the same time, Neptune can inspire you and bolster your imagination, so your creative endeavors are more fruitful. Depending on its position at one's birth, Neptune can influence people to grow up into great artists. Still, its confusing, illusory nature can also make an individual prone to escapism and uncertainty.

Pluto

- **Color:** Dark red
- **Stones:** Red jasper
- **Keywords:** Evolution, death, power, transformation

Pluto has had many glyphs used to represent it by astronomers, astrologers, and other observers. One of the more common glyphs consists of a bident that rests upon a cross base, with a small circle known as Pluto's orb between the two prongs on top. The bident symbolizes the bident of Hades, the Greek god of the underworld, later renamed Pluto. This glyph is the one typically used in astrology. Still, another common symbol representing this dwarf planet is a simple monogram made up of the letters "P" and "L," representing the initials of Percival Lowell, the planet's discoverer.

Being the most distant sometimes-planet in our solar system, Pluto takes between twelve and fifteen years to transition between zodiac signs. The dwarf planet also goes through a retrograde cycle between April 29 and October 8, 2022. The planet is exalted when in the sign of Aries, in fall in Leo, and in detriment when in Taurus. Even though associated with the god of death and the underworld, Pluto is regarded as the planet of rebirth and transformation. Pluto's energy is a regenerative force for people and the world. Like other slow-transitioning planets, Pluto is an influence that manifests slowly across generations, more often than immediately in an individual's life. As such, it's a subtle influence, but its energy can lead to great transformations in the long run.

Chapter 3: Know More with Nodes and Asteroids

After acquainting yourself with the basic bits of info regarding the planets through our brief introduction in the previous chapter, it's time to explore a few other aspects of deeper astrology. Nodes and asteroids, for instance, are additional factors that play important roles in more sophisticated and accurate astrological readings, particularly when making your birth chart, which we'll touch upon later in the book. Practical astrology is all about getting as much information as possible regarding the astrological circumstances of a person's birth and life, and the often-overlooked concepts like nodes and asteroids will go a long way.

Nodes

While your zodiac sign or astrological houses are there to give insight into your personality and help you learn things about yourself, lunar nodes have a somewhat different purpose. In the simplest terms and most, the purpose of analyzing your lunar nodes is to gain insights into the future. More precisely, nodes can help you discover your purpose in life and what long-term goals you should focus on. Like everything else in astrology, these nodes aren't an exact science. They won't predict your future like a crystal ball, but analyzing them can give you quite a few useful ideas and hints that can help you make your own conclusions as you go along.

Lunar nodes are usually analyzed as part of a birth chart reading, where the reader analyzes the ecliptic's movement and axis at the time of your birth, among other things. Lunar nodes include the north node and the south node, each associated with certain aspects of the future and past. They're all about the path you walk in life, focusing not just on the experiences and decisions you're going to make but also on things like learning and growth in the broadest sense. For this reason, the nodes are also often referred to as the Nodes of Fate.

When observing a typical birth chart, you'll notice that the north and south nodes are on opposite sides. The first thing to note is that these nodes aren't celestial bodies like planets or stars. They are mathematically determined points, and, on a birth chart, they end up on two zodiac signs opposite each other. These mathematical points depend on the relationship between the sun, moon, and Earth when you were born. The mathematical side of calculating the position of the nodes can get a bit complicated. Still, birth chart generators and expert astrologers will determine them based on the information concerning your birth. Suffice it to say that the nodes on your birth chart will fall where the moon's monthly path and the sun's yearly path across the zodiac meet. In general, people turn to their lunar nodes when they are tormented by questions concerning what they should do in life or their purpose, both narrow and broad. However, nodes can also give you insight into how you ended up where you already are by looking into the past, perhaps even beyond this life.

In simple terms, the south node is about where you're coming from, while the north node is about where you're going, particularly in this life. Even though they are separate, the two lunar nodes are also intricately connected, so reading one without the other is futile. They feed into and depend on each other, just as your future can often be connected to your past, at least because the past must be overcome to move on.

Since the south node concerns the things you bring into this life from the start, it's associated with gifts and baggage, be it emotional, karmic, or any other kind. On the other hand, the north node brings opportunities to overcome that baggage and grow out of our limitations to alter our path in life for the better. The nodes are also sometimes called the Dragon's Tail (south node) and the Dragon's Head (north node).

Many astrologers will refer to the north node as the individual's "karmic destiny" in the current life. It represents the end goal you're moving toward, which ultimately depends on the lessons of past lives. As such, the north node isn't about analyzing your character and personality but is entirely focused on predicting future outcomes. Many astrologers see the north node as something that's naturally difficult to deal with, which is why people often don't tackle the true meaning of their north node until they're in their thirties. When dealing with the future, the north node is also often associated with the unknown, naturally producing unease and anxiety in people.

The best way to tackle the implications of your north node is to try and incorporate the qualities of its sign on the chart. Since the south node concerns all those things you already are, it's naturally a more comfortable place. It's no accident that the nodes fall on opposite sides of the chart, as there is quite a leap between them. The north node entails many qualities that feel foreign at first glance, but those are the things you need to focus on to improve yourself and your life. Practically speaking, it's all about analyzing the sign and house of the north node to figure out which aspects of your life and personality you need to work on.

Those aspects are all those issues you'd rather avoid and escape from instead of dealing with them. They're areas where you know you need to improve but haven't yet mustered the strength to do so. And since many people aren't even in a place where they know what exactly they need to change, this is precisely what the north node can reveal to them. Embracing the north node and heeding its guidance is the first step toward getting a handle on your destiny and attaining the sense of purpose that comes from understanding your nodes.

As you can see, the south node is the opposite of the north node in many ways. This node is your base, representing everything you already know and have mastered. It's your comfort zone, familiar territory, and a place to fall back to when the going gets tough. None of this suggests that it's less important, but the objective is to build upon this foundation and grow into the person you want to become. Having the south node to fall back on is good as long as this doesn't turn into avoidance and passivity.

When it comes to the moon, another subject worth noting is something called Black Moon Lilith. This astrological concept is usually analyzed by astrologers who are a bit more advanced than average with the hope of revealing a few other things about you and your life. Lilith mostly concerns those things that lay hidden, such as your dark sexual desires or any other hidden aspects of yourself. In the simplest terms, Black Moon Lilith represents the most distant point on the moon's orbit around Earth. Lilith's primary associations include primitive impulses, instincts, repressed desires and thoughts, the subconscious, and one's true, hidden self in its rawest form. Some astrologers refer to this as our "shadow self."

Asteroids

As we briefly mentioned earlier, astrological influences come from more than just the planets and the constellations. Asteroids play an important but often overlooked role in your astrological destiny. Thus, it is necessary to get at least a basic understanding of what they are in an astrological sense, which ones you should look out for, and exactly what they represent. Certain comets and meteors can also play important roles. By analyzing all of these factors, astrological readings can give you much more insight than the typical, shallow analysis you'd find in a daily horoscope. Even with expert astrologers, you might sometimes find that the main planets just don't say enough to help you answer some of the burning questions in your very unique, specific story. That's why it's important to consider all those additional layers provided by asteroids, comets, and other phenomena.

Similar to how astrology classifies the sun and the moon as "planets," the classification of "asteroids" includes those other two groups of celestial bodies we just mentioned. There are a few asteroids to look at, depending on how deep you want to delve into reading. Some asteroids are more influential and revered than others, so it's good to know which ones to focus on if you're in a rush to read a chart as fast as possible. Some of the most common asteroids to look out for include:

- Ceres
- Chiron
- Pallas
- Juno
- Vesta
- Eros
- Sappho
- Psyche
- Eris
- Pholus
- Sedna

- Chariklo

- Haumea

- Makemake

- Hygeia

Ceres is an asteroid or, more precisely, a dwarf planet that radiates a loving, nurturing energy resembling the force of maternity. It's a valuable pointer in chart readings because it reveals things about the tender parts of our nature, teaching us how we may become more nurturing and loving to those around us while also helping us realize what it is we need in life to feel the same being reciprocated. Ceres was named after the Roman goddess of agriculture and is intricately connected to the earth, sustenance, and nurturance themes. Ceres is also associated with life's natural cycles, including birth and death.

Chiron is also referred to as the wound healer, emphasizing healing and overcoming trauma and pain that follow an individual through life. Chiron's name comes from Greek mythology, particularly the centaur Chiron. This half-man and half-horse was a healer, but he sustained a wound that he couldn't heal, leaving him to suffer for eternity until he was given rest among the stars. Chiron's destiny is a powerful symbol of what this asteroid is all about. It represents your weakest point and that small bustle of pain you may be carrying, which is unique to you. Chiron's power lies in showing you how to overcome that painful wound and teaching others to overcome theirs.

Pallas has an energy that resembles that of Mars in some respects. This asteroid and its associated deity are also referred to as Pallas Athena, and its primary areas of influence include things like strategy, wisdom, and intellectual pursuits. In Greek mythology, Pallas was also the sister of Ares (Mars). She represented a more rational, restrained influence associated with warfare and justice and wisdom in struggle, in contrast to the highly aggressive nature of her brother. The influence of Pallas manifests in things like leadership, a sense of justice, conflict resolution, and relationships, especially with authority figures and fathers.

According to ancient Greek mythology, Juno bears the name of the sister-wife of Zeus (Jupiter), the queen of Olympus and the goddess of marriage. Juno's energy is one of commitment and loyalty but also of vindictiveness. In mythology, Juno's quiet fury and drive for vengeance stemmed from the constant infidelity of Zeus. This is why, at the very least, the astrological influence of Juno has a lot to do with relationships, particularly marriage, and how it fares against the harsh realities of life. Juno's guidance can help you reach certain realizations about your marital and familial relationships, for better or for worse.

Vesta, which is a dwarf planet, is the asteroid of spirituality. In ancient Rome, Vesta was associated with the spring equinox, the start of the year, and the ritual fires lit by the Romans to celebrate this time of year. In a way, Vesta was also seen as a keeper of these sacred fires. Vesta was also a virgin goddess, so there are strong associations with purity and incorruptibility. Vesta's energy is also one of self-determination and self-ownership, which is why it can strengthen the influence of the astrological house it occupies or a planet or sign it interacts with.

Eros is also known as Cupid, the son of Venus in mythology. As a distinguished seducer and the god of desire, he was known as the god who married princess Psyche in a somewhat peculiar arrangement where he would only interact with her in complete darkness, never revealing himself. Because of this, the asteroid Eros has a lot to do with sexuality. By extension, there are also strong associations with passion and desire. Eros can reveal to us our inner desires, usually regarding sexuality but not exclusively. Sometimes, Eros can also influence particularly strong desires in other areas of life, related to work, relationships, and much else.

Psyche, in Greek mythology, was a mortal princess of immense beauty, as described in the story of Psyche and Cupid (Eros). Psyche's beauty was so awe-inspiring that it even made the goddess Aphrodite seethe with jealousy, which was why she sent her son, Cupid, to poison her. However, when faced with her beauty, Eros falls in love, and that's how their relationship began. If Eros represents your desires and preferences in sexuality, then Psyche does the same regarding emotional satisfaction and bonding. Psyche influences your choice of who you're willing to commit to and, as such, has sway over romantic relationships.

Sappho bears the name of an ancient Greek poet who lived and wrote on the Greek island of Lesbos. Much of her poetry had to do with eroticism, particularly in same-sex relationships. This asteroid's energy is one of harmony, closeness, and care between lovers. It's also associated with solidarity and belonging, often guiding you toward finding your place of affirmation, understanding, and belonging. Sappho's energy affects professional and intimate relationships, so its positioning in your birth chart can shed light on many important things in your life.

Eris is a dwarf planet, and, like an asteroid in astrology, it's something of a counterpart to Eros. Named after the Greek goddess of discord, Eris, who was equal to the Roman Discordia, Eris radiates powerful feminine energy that carries quite a bit of aggression and anger, although righteously so. This is one of the astrological forces that give us the fuel to rebel. Eris can shed light on where and why in your life you feel the need to stand up in protest and rebellion, which can be quite pronounced in some of the more rebellious signs of the zodiac, such as the aggressive and stubborn Aries.

Pholus bears the name of a centaur, like Chiron. In Greek mythology, both of these centaurs were unusually gentle creatures relative to others of their kind. In the myths, Pholus usually spent his days guarding vineyards and living in a cave until an attack left him poisoned by an arrow, ultimately leading to his death. This is why much of the energy of Pholus is sacrificial, denoting our willingness to help others even at a considerable personal cost. Pholus is also associated with wine, poisons, and intoxication, followed by a loss of control. This asteroid also reveals ways to help others heal their wounds, even if we do so unintentionally. Because of its particularly long orbit of around 92 years, Pholus's influence is mostly trans-generational.

Sedna is an asteroid with an incredibly wide orbit around the sun, so wide that astronomers barely noticed it. The orbit spans well beyond our solar system, and Sedna's orbital period takes thousands of years. One of Sedna's powers is to show us all those good things in life, which we can focus on to help us feel better about our shortcomings and failures. The asteroid is strongly associated with blessings and motivates us to make the best of every gift instead of making excuses and falling into despair.

Chariklo is strongly associated with the centaur Chiron in mythology. She was a nymph who married Chariklo and was a daughter to Apollo. She was also a sort of mentor to some of the most legendary heroes in Greek mythology, including the mighty Achilles. Chariklo was also seen as a faithful and devoted wife, which is why some of this asteroid's strongest associations include caretaking and supportiveness. This asteroid is generally associated with personal space, healing, and awakening.

Haumea is a dwarf planet identified in 2004 and named after the Hawaiian goddess of childbirth and fertility. In Hawaiian mythology, she was said to have given birth to many children by making them from parts of her body. She was also said to have taken many physical forms and been reborn many times. Haumea infuses us with love for the natural world around us, which helps us feel connected to nature. This asteroid also shows us how to overcome adversity and obstacles that life may throw in our way.

Makemake is another dwarf planet discovered in 2005, just a year after Haumea. The origin of this asteroid's name is quite exotic, as it comes from the creator god worshiped by the people of Easter Island. Some of this asteroid's themes are similar to those of Haumea, including the love of nature. This energy helps us see the beauty in all things around us and reminds us that nature is something we have to care for. In your chart, Makemake is an influence that will help you manifest your desires more easily in the real world.

Hygeia represents the asteroid of wellness, as it's usually called. In Greek and Roman myths, she was the daughter of Asclepius, the god of medicine. Just as her father's symbol lives on through the serpent on a staff that's so often used in medicine today, Hygeia's name also lives on through the word "hygiene," which is derived from it. Hygeia was also one of five sisters who symbolized different aspects of human health care, and her area of expertise was prevention. This asteroid shows us how to properly care for ourselves to ensure we remain in good mental and physical health.

Chapter 4: The 12 Zodiac Signs

Zodiac circle.

https://pixabay.com/images/id-5921179/

Being versed in all zodiac signs and their properties is another important step toward becoming more proficient in astrology. Apart from giving you a better understanding of other people and how to relate to them, understanding all twelve signs will be important for your personal readings. This is because each individual has three signs, including the sun, moon, and rising (ascendant) sign.

People usually look at the sun sign for simplistic astrological readings if they don't want to dig that deep, but knowing all three of your signs will be very important for deeper insight. Remember that your moon sign will be the zodiac sign in which the moon was located at the time of your birth, which will usually be different from your sun sign. On the other hand, the ascendant sign is the sign that was on the horizon at that same time. Knowing all three of your signs is necessary for things like birth chart readings, but more on that later. For now, we'll go through a brief overview of all twelve zodiac signs and what makes them special.

Aries

- **Date:** March 21 – April 19
- **Keywords:** Courage, confidence, will, initiation, first, vitality, conquest, hunter.
- **Mantra:** "I am."
- **Planetary Rulership:** Mars
- **Color:** Red
- **Metal:** Iron
- **Birthstone:** Diamond
- **Body Part:** Head

Aries is symbolized by the Ram, whose glyph illustrates its distinct horns. The symbolism of the Ram and its horns is no coincidence, as it reflects Aries's headstrong and confrontational nature. Unsurprisingly, the sign's element is fire to those who know an Aries. This powerful and intense element feeds much of the strength, energy, and confidence that Rams are renowned for. The sign's modality is cardinal, and it's the first of the four cardinal signs. Aries' position as the first cardinal sign and its date range, which begins with the start of spring, are important factors that define the Ram as a leader and initiator.

The Ram's positive polarity is another aspect that can help you understand this sign better, as it's clearly in line with how Aries interacts with the world. Like other positive signs, Aries focuses its energy outward and tends to be a sign that likes to express itself, as opposed to signs with negative polarity, which are receptive and more inward-oriented when it comes to focusing their energy. Remember that this sign's energies, like any other, will play a certain part in your life, even if it's just your moon or ascendant sign. Aries can be hotheaded at times, but they are natural-born leaders and initiators who can do wonderful things for others and for themselves in life.

Taurus

- **Date:** April 20 – May 20
- **Keywords:** Stable, security, possessions, money, loyalty, stubborn, indulgence, pleasure.
- **Mantra:** "I have."
- **Planetary Rulership:** Venus (Classic) and Ceres (Modern)
- **Color:** Green, pink
- **Metal:** Copper
- **Birthstone:** Emerald
- **Body Part:** Throat

The bull and its namesake constellation symbolize Taurus. The sign is represented by a glyph that consists of a simple circle with two horns on top, symbolizing the bull and its characteristic traits, such as stubbornness. Taurus is an earth sign regarding elements, and this heaviest of all elements in astrology is a powerful symbol of the bull's stability, patience, solidity, and strength.

The Bull is a sign possessing a fixed modality, and it's the first such sign in the zodiac. Much of the stability and perseverance that fixed signs enjoy comes from the fact that they occupy middle positions concerning their respective seasons, such as the Bull's poisoning in the middle of spring. Taureans are known for their ability to relentlessly pursue their goals and their principles regardless of outside pressure, and their fixed modality plays a big role in that trait. Taurus is also a negative sign concerning its polarity, which is one of the reasons many Taureans end up as fairly introverted, quietly strong types. Taureans are also known for their love of pleasure and all the finer things in life, which can veer off into hedonism if unchecked. Bulls can also often benefit from the artistic and affectionate energies of Venus, their ruling planet.

Gemini

- **Date:** May 21 – June 20
- **Keywords:** Inquisitive, curious, intelligence, wit, mischief, learning, communication.
- **Mantra:** "I think."
- **Planetary Rulership:** Mercury
- **Color:** Yellow, light green
- **Metal:** Bronze
- **Birthstone:** Emerald, tiger's eye
- **Body Part:** Lungs, arms, hands

Gemini, symbolized by the Twins, is represented by a glyph consisting of two equal parts joined together in perfect symmetry, resembling the Roman number two. The story of the Twins has its roots in Greek mythology and the story of Pollux and Castor, two brothers born to Leda. Pairs are a common theme in the lives of many Geminis, and both the Twin symbol and the sign's glyph illustrate that quite well.

Gemini is a sign of elemental air, the lightest element, which is one of the factors responsible for Gemini's highly dynamic and outgoing nature. They are folks who live to be on the move, always learning and experiencing new things and meeting new people. Geminis are also highly curious and, sometimes, no strangers to mischief. Regarding modality, Gemini is the first of the mutable signs, which further strengthens the sign's highly dynamic temperament and makes it very adaptable. Unsurprisingly, this outgoing and outwardly oriented sign has a positive polarity and shows all the time. The moon sign of Gemini can make some of the sign's traits particularly intense, making such individuals a bit too outgoing and open at times. The same goes for ascendant Geminis, who are prone to restlessness.

Cancer

- **Date:** June 21 – July 22
- **Keywords:** Intuitive, nurturing, caring, sensitive, protective, selfless.
- **Mantra:** "I feel."

- **Planetary Rulership:** The Moon
- **Color:** White, violet
- **Metal:** Iron
- **Birthstone:** Pearl, ruby
- **Body Part:** Breast, brain, stomach

Cancer, also known as the Crab, is a sign represented by a glyph that doesn't exactly correspond to the appearance of the symbolic animal. It's a symmetrical glyph that resembles two commas or nines positioned into a circular shape. The meaning of the symbol has been the object of some speculation. Some astrologers suggest it might have been intended as a symbol of breasts to signify Cancer's nurturing, maternal nature.

Cancer's element is water, which infuses the sign with enough fluidity to make it adaptable while providing more weight than air, making Cancers more grounded and reserved than Geminis. This is the second among cardinal signs, heralding the beginning of summer and drawing this energy's strength of leadership and initiative. The intensity of the sun's energy during this time is also a major source of this strength. Nonetheless, Cancer's polarity is negative since, despite the sign's capacity to be authoritative and to lead, the Crab retains a significant degree of introspection and quietness. The Crab's nurturing, caring, and sacrificial nature is especially pronounced in moon Cancers since it's the sign's ruling planet. Such Cancers can be prone to being nurturing and committed to others to a fault and a point where it becomes detrimental to them due to self-neglect.

Leo

- **Date:** July 23 – August 22
- **Keywords:** Proud, artistic, expressive, creative, leadership, performance, radiating.
- **Mantra:** "I will."
- **Planetary Rulership:** The Sun
- **Color:** Yellow, orange, gold
- **Metal:** Bronze
- **Birthstone:** Carnelian
- **Body Part:** Heart

Leo is symbolized by the Lion, which perfectly encapsulates its proud, regal, and imposing nature. The sign's glyph consists of a small circle and an attached curved line, and it can resemble the head of a lion and his mane or a tail, depending on how you look at it. Either way, the sign's symbol animal says more than plenty about the nature of Leos.

If you have a Leo in your life, none of the astrological factors influencing this sign will likely be surprising. For one thing, the sign is infused with the energy of elemental fire, giving Leos the endless supply of strength and pep they need to get out there and impress others through their signature shine. Regarding modality, the Lion is the second among fixed signs, which is yet another source of the sign's strength, stability, and authority. Leos find themselves positioned right in the middle of summer when the sun is at its very peak concerning the light, warmth, and energy that it radiates. Of course, Leo is a positive sign and lives to interact, attract, impress, and shine within any group. The moon in Leo can often limit the sign's pride, ego, and outgoing character, which can be just the balance that some of the more intense Leos need.

Virgo

- **Date:** August 23 – September 22
- **Keywords:** Order, systematic, analytical, practical, discerning, critical, precise.
- **Mantra:** "I analyze."
- **Planetary Rulership:** Mercury (Classic) and Chiron (Modern)
- **Color:** Beige, silver
- **Metal:** Bronze
- **Birthstone:** Peridot
- **Body Part:** Digestive tract

Virgo, also known as *the Maiden*, has one of the more intricate glyphs in the zodiac, communicating several meanings to the viewer. For one, it clearly resembles a cursive letter "M," but the glyph's intricate design, which sports numerous lines, also points to the fact that this sign relates to our intestines and our digestive system. The ends of the glyph's lines that curve inward are also symbolic of the sign's introspective and analytical nature.

Virgo's modality is mutable, making it the second such sign and giving it an aura of adaptability and an ability to handle changes very well. The gradually weakening sun in the final stage of summer, which Virgo occupies, can also be a significant influence that makes Virgos more restrained and reserved. Virgo is a well-balanced sign because its mutable modality is countered by its earth element, making Virgos grounded and solid. This sign is also negative in polarity, another factor responsible for Virgo's discerning, analytical, and critical nature. Virgos are also renowned for their organizational skills and tend to be very tidy. These are excellent virtues as long as Virgos ensures they don't become obsessive and overly caught up in small details while failing to grasp wider concepts and the bigger picture.

Libra

- **Date:** September 23 – October 22
- **Keywords:** Beauty, harmony, peace, art, diplomacy, compromise, balance.
- **Mantra:** "I relate."
- **Planetary Rulership:** Venus
- **Color:** Green, blue
- **Metal:** Copper
- **Birthstone:** Sapphire
- **Body Part:** Kidneys, lower back

Seeing as though the Scales symbolize Libras, their glyph is mostly straightforward. It's a perfectly symmetrical glyph that resembles the scales of justice, making Libra one of the few signs whose symbols don't involve animals. Nonetheless, the celestial symbol and the glyph perfectly illustrate Libra's passion for harmony, balance, and justice.

Libras tend to be outgoing, highly dynamic, and energetic folks, thanks in part to their element of air. However, this sign is the third among cardinal signs of the zodiac. It is positioned at the beginning of autumn when the sun's energy begins to diminish more noticeably. This gives Libra a degree of calm and control that prevents them from getting too intense. The autumn equinox is one of the factors contributing to Libra's capacity and craving for balance. Balance comes into all aspects of Libra's worldview and lifestyle, influencing everything from their passion for justice to their ability to be diplomats and make compromises. Because of this, Libra is a positive sign that's ultimately oriented toward the outer world, despite being more restrained than most Geminis, for instance. Most Libras are highly social and tend to be the most elegant and well-spoken in most groups they find themselves in.

Scorpio

- **Date:** October 23 – November 21
- **Keywords:** Focus, drive, ambition, determination, persistence, intensity, emotion.
- **Mantra:** "I transform."
- **Planetary Rulership:** Mars (Classic) and Pluto (Modern)
- **Color:** Red, black
- **Metal:** Iron
- **Birthstone:** Opal, topaz
- **Body Part:** Bowels, genitals

As is well known and quite clear at first glance, the Scorpion symbolizes Scorpio. Also, the sign's glyph seems very straightforward at first glance since the first thing most people notice is the scorpion tail on its right side. Upon further inspection, it quickly becomes apparent that there's more to this glyph than meets the eye. The tail is a curved line with an arrow at the end, protruding from the right end of an M-shape. In general, the threatening scorpion tail the glyph contains is a powerful symbol of the intensity and useful aggression inherent to this sign.

Scorpio's stability and determination are partly due to it being the third fixed sign of the zodiac. The sign's position in the middle of autumn also has much to do with its reflective, reserved, quiet, and introspective nature. Scorpios can be the epitome of strength in silence. At the same time, elemental water is a dynamic influence in the Scorpion's life, responsible for creativity, imagination, and drive. Being one of the zodiac's most reserved and inward-oriented signs, it's unsurprising that Scorpio possesses a negative polarity. Despite the Scorpion's tendency to be reserved and consumed by their inner world, this sign is emotionally sophisticated and more than capable of feeling, regardless of how unexpressive Scorpio might seem.

Sagittarius

- **Date:** November 22 – December 21
- **Keywords:** Learning, novelty, travel, philosophy, question, teaching, searching.
- **Mantra:** "I see."
- **Planetary Rulership:** Jupiter
- **Color:** Blue, light blue
- **Metal:** Gunmetal
- **Birthstone:** Topaz
- **Body Part:** Thighs, liver, hips

Sagittarius is known as and symbolized by the Archer. This sign has one of the most straightforward glyphs, consisting of an arrow with a short line striking it in half, symbolizing the Archer's bow and arrow. The arrow is inclined toward the right at 45 degrees, pointing to the northeast. This direction can be interpreted as the arrow pointing away into the distance, symbolizing the Archer's inherent thirst for adventure, discovery, and learning.

Sagittarius is a fire sign, perfectly in line with the Archer's drive and endless energy to fuel their adventurism. These dynamic folks can even get carried away in their search for novelty and truth, veering off into the territory of recklessness. However, their mutable modality helps Sagittarians improvise, adapt, and overcome obstacles, usually ending up fine despite the odds. The Archer occupies a position at the end of autumn, with the sign's date range ending just as winter takes hold. This is the energy that helps Archers transform and adapt to changes. This highly outgoing and world-oriented sign has a positive polarity and can often leave an impression on others. Sagittarians are highly expressive and blunt to a fault, never afraid to call things as they see them, even if that means stating some uncomfortable truths.

Capricorn

- **Date:** December 22 – January 19
- **Keywords:** Diligence, practical, loner, goals, structure, conservative, ambition, work, efficiency.

- **Mantra:** "I use."
- **Planetary Rulership:** Saturn
- **Color:** Brown, black, dark blue
- **Metal:** Gunmetal
- **Birthstone:** Lapis lazuli
- **Body Part:** Knees

Capricorn, also known as the Sea-Goat of the zodiac, has by far the most intricate and complex glyph that consists of two symbols placed side-by-side. The left piece is usually interpreted as a goat's head, while the right resembles a seagoing tail that might be found on a fish or a mythical creature such as a mermaid. However, the complexity of the glyph allows for some interpretation.

Capricorns draw strength and solidity from the influence of their earthy element. Sea-Goats are strong, stable, hardworking, goal-oriented, and often authoritative. It's not uncommon for Capricorns to occupy positions of power or responsibility for other people, in which they tend to feel right at home. Capricorn is the last of the cardinal signs, and it's positioned at the start of winter, which further influences the sign's leadership potential. Capricorns tend to be the kind of people who command respect in all settings and crowds because of how they relate to others and carry themselves. Even though Capricorns have a negative polarity and are prone to solitude and introspection, they often aren't all that sensitive. Many Capricorns find it hard to express themselves and open up to other people on any meaningful level. This works out fine for most of them since they are more than capable of solving their own problems, but they may miss out on valuable help that could have otherwise made their lives much easier.

Aquarius

- **Date:** January 20 – February 18
- **Keywords:** Intelligence, social, detachment, individuality, rebel, logical.
- **Mantra:** "I know."
- **Planetary Rulership:** Saturn (Classic) and Uranus (Modern)
- **Color:** Sky blue

- **Metal:** Copper
- **Birthstone:** Amethyst
- **Body Part:** Shins

Aquarius is symbolized and recognized as the Water Bearer, and its glyph perfectly complements that fact. The two parallel, wavy lines of this glyph follow closely with the theme of the sign's celestial symbol, even though Aquarius is unexpectedly an air sign. Still, the symbolism of water and the way it flows does suggest something about this sign's ability to communicate freely and engage with people.

This sign's air element allows Aquarians to think so freely and originally, helping them come up with all those innovative ideas they're known for. Aquarians are also adept at improvisation and find it easy to stay on top of things no matter how many curveballs fly their way. This is the last fixed sign regarding modality and is situated right in the dead of winter, providing the perfect counterbalance to elemental air and its influence. Aquarians are generally outgoing, and their polarity is positive, making them one of the most balanced signs when it comes to keeping their inner world of ideas and communication with the outside world on an even scale. All of these factors are why Aquarians often find themselves in the field of science or lifelong academic careers.

Pisces

- **Date:** February 19 – March 20
- **Keywords:** Compassion, intuition, creativity, spirituality, dreamer, adaptable, imagination.
- **Mantra:** "I believe."
- **Planetary Rulership:** Jupiter (Classic) and Neptune (Modern)
- **Color:** Purple, violet, sea green
- **Metal:** Gunmetal
- **Birthstone:** Moonstone
- **Body Part:** Liver, feet

The Fish symbolizes Pisces, and its glyph shows a connection to that symbol. Another symmetrical glyph consists of two lines that curve away from each other and almost touch the tips in the middle of the two curves, where one horizontal line strikes through both of them. Illustrations of the

Fish often portray the same symbolism by having the fish swimming in opposite directions. One way to interpret this is as a symbol of the Pisces' constant pursuit of ideals that they have to balance with the realities of the outside world. This inner conflict is the struggle of this sign's life, but it's also the source of everything we love about Pisces.

Pisces is the last mutable sign, and, as such, the Fish tends to be adaptable and capable of improvisation in rapidly changing conditions. The dynamic nature of Pisces is further consolidated by its element of water and the act that it falls at the end of winter. It doesn't herald the start of a season, but it certainly relates to a time of natural transformation. At the same time, Pisces is a negative sign that focuses much of its energy and emotions on its inner world. The Fish is intuitive, spiritual, and prone to dream big. Despite this inward focus, Pisces is one of the most compassionate signs you can meet, always having a lot of understanding for other people and their predicaments.

Chapter 5: Going through the 12 Houses

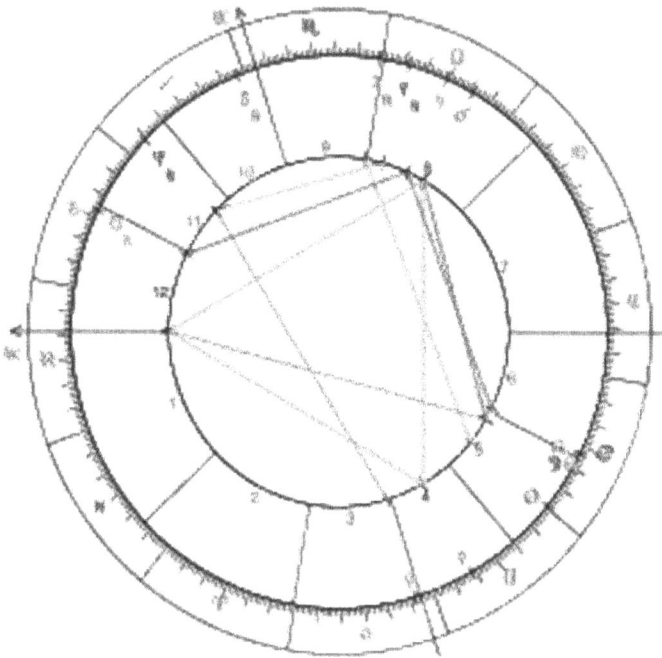

House Wheel.

Morn, CC BY-SA 3.0 <https://creativecommons.org/licenses/by-sa/3.0>, via Wikimedia Commons
https://commons.wikimedia.org/wiki/File:Natal_Chart_-_Adam.svg

Astrological *houses* constitute another important aspect of astrological reading that's especially useful in creating and properly interpreting birth charts. Along with zodiac signs, planets, and planetary aspects, these houses are the basis of every birth chart. Throughout history, different cultures and astrological disciplines have come up with a few different systems, but the most frequently used approach in Western astrology nowadays is the Placidus system.

There are twelve astrological houses, which correspond to a twelve-part division of the ecliptic plane of our sun's orbit. It's essentially a division of the zodiac from east to west on the horizon based on the observation location. This is why your rising sign will fall on the left side of the zodiac, the eastern horizon. In simple terms, these twelve houses are the twelve equal parts or areas that you'll see on most horoscope wheels, and you'll find that each is occupied by one of the twelve zodiac signs. This division of the horoscope into twelve parts depends on the rotation of the Earth and the precise place and time of an individual's birth rather than just the date.

Each of the houses influences a certain area of your life, and the position of the planets and zodiac signs regarding these houses at the exact time of your birth can determine aspects of your personality and experience in this life through a combination of astrological influences that's fairly unique to you. This chapter will take a quick overview of the twelve houses, what they represent, and how they influence us.

The House of Self

- **Keywords:** Self, identity, appearance, ego, personality, attitude, wellness, beginning
- **Ruling Sign:** Aries
- **Planet:** Mars

The first house is the house of identity, ego, beginnings, and all things that are first. In birth charts, this is the house where the ascendant sign shows up over the horizon as you are born. Perhaps the most defining characteristic of the first astrological house is that it's entirely devoted to describing you and your personality. The house is also associated with your body, including your physical appearance and how you feel within your own skin. This makes it different from other houses because they generally refer to things, places, and people you'll encounter and experience throughout your life, all of which are external factors. Simply put, the first house is the fountainhead of your identity, through which it can affect all aspects of your life.

How the first house will affect your identity will be further modified by the planet that finds itself in this particular house at your birth. This is how planetary influences with their unique energies interact with the twelve houses, creating a combination of astrological influences unique to you. Since the first house is all about identity, it's up to you or an astrologer to interpret how each of the planets might fit into the equation, as you'll learn a bit later. For now, consider the example of Mercury, which is a planet known for its expressive energy and association with communication. If your birth chart shows that Mercury was in your first house at birth, you might find that you like to talk and are highly communicative.

The House of Possessions

- **Keywords:** Value, possessions, earning, self-esteem, money, security, work, routines
- **Ruling Sign:** Taurus
- **Planet:** Venus

The second house is the house of possessions, value, or income, among other names. These names suggest what area of life this house is associated with. This house governs the number of material possessions you have and financial stability. The second house can also affect the stability of other areas of your life, especially those in your immediate surroundings. The second house's association with value also goes into a more abstract realm, affecting your inner value system. This can translate into how you prioritize things in life or how much you care about material possessions. This is how you decide your needs and wants in life, including the differences between failure and success or happiness and misery.

The second house can be responsible for shaping entire mentalities concerning money and resources, influencing things like scarcity mentality, irresponsible spending, or habits like hoarding. The way you value material things, relationships, and ultimately yourself are all areas that the second house affects. It's important to consider how individual planets might steer these influences in several directions, either to your benefit or detriment. Saturn, for instance, is a force of discipline and order, so its presence in the second house tends to make us financially responsible.

The House of Sharing

- **Keywords:** Environment, siblings, communication, mind, social, early education
- **Ruling Sign:** Gemini
- **Planet:** Mercury

The house of sharing or communication is the third of the twelve houses, and it's the home of Gemini. As its name suggests, this house is about how you communicate and interact with others. It's also associated with how you communicate with yourself, which means that this house affects how you think and resonate, having to do with your inner monologue, thoughts, and introspection. Having said all that, the third house can exert tremendous influence on your ability to fit in with teams, communities, neighborhoods, friends, and family. This influence can thus dictate the nature and quality of relationships. Other areas of life that this house can affect include how you do at school in your early years, including how you acquire skills and basic knowledge.

Humans are social animals, and communication is one of the most important facets of existence. Problems in this area can lead to failure in communication, which can have untold consequences in every walk of life, from home to work to friendship. Bearing this in mind, you need to be wary of any planets that might find themselves transiting through your third house at birth, as these can be a source of great strength or a problem you need to work on in life.

The House of Home and Family

- **Keywords:** Home, family, emotions, children, mothers, femininity, roots
- **Ruling Sign:** Cancer
- **Planet:** The Moon

While the third house focuses on communication more generally, the fourth house is more exclusively focused on family life and all affairs relating to your home. This influence doesn't just flow into your current, immediate family but also to relatives and your ancestors. It's no surprise that a sign as nurturing and home-oriented as Cancer finds its home in this house, as the two complement each other perfectly.

The fourth house is responsible for your sense of belonging to a place and to people you are connected to via your roots. This energy feeds the human ability to acknowledge and value continuity through generations, a type of awareness unique to us as a species. Home also means security and a sense of shelter; the fourth house is where this warmth resides. Of course, this house will also affect how you perceive family life and how much importance you ascribe to it. As such, it's important to consider any planets that might have passed through the fourth house at birth. The loving and beautifying energy of Venus, for instance, tends to strengthen our familial bonds. In contrast, some of the more aggressive planetary energies can lead to hot tempers in the home.

The House of Pleasure

- **Keywords:** Romance, love, creativity, fertility, expression, joy, fun, risk

- **Ruling Sign:** Leo

- **Planet:** The Sun

The house of pleasure is another astrological house with a pretty self-explanatory name regarding the central theme. All those things that please you in life have to do with this house and its influences. Still, there's more to it than meets the eye, as the fifth house also has to do with creation in the broadest sense. This means that it's associated with things like procreation and birth, art, and other creative endeavors. Similar to the second house of value, the fifth house affects your perception since our ideas of pleasure are open to quite a bit of variation from one individual to the next.

In a broader sense, the placement of planets in your fifth house can determine how much importance you give to pleasure. For instance, if a planet like Venus finds itself traversing through your fifth house at birth, you are likely to be the kind of person who sees no point in life without all sorts of pleasure. Other placements or a lack thereof might lead you in the opposite direction in life. The fifth house is also connected with risk-taking, particularly regarding pleasure and indulgence, so it's important to be wary of those planetary influences getting out of hand. If you act accordingly, you'll find a way to ensure a safe balance between risk and reward, especially with the help of more restraining influences like Saturn.

The House of Health

- **Keywords:** Health, fitness, analysis, nature, work routines, organization, utility
- **Ruling Sign:** Virgo
- **Planet:** Mercury

The sixth house is commonly referred to as the house of health and sometimes as the house of maintenance. This house is the source of our vitality, strength, and overall wellness, especially physical. On the flip side, the sixth house is also associated with disease and injury or, more precisely, how we deal with these obstacles to our well-being. In general, much of this house's energy revolves around daily struggles in all forms and intensity levels, depending on an individual's life. Because of the association with struggle daily, Mars can make for an interesting combination with this house because of its aggressive energy and its ancient association with war.

Planets that energize things like discipline, routine, and self-care can positively influence them if they enter this house at birth. Such a combination of energies can make it easier to adopt healthy habits and avoid bad ones. The house is also strongly associated with routines and work-related duties. This house's connection to well-being also goes beyond just physical health; its energy can be the driving force behind self-improvement and growth in the broadest sense.

The House of Balance

- **Keywords:** Relationships, marriage, sharing, contracts, partnerships
- **Ruling Sign:** Libra
- **Planet:** Venus

The house of balance, also known as the house of partnerships, is where Libra finds its home. The association with partnership has wide implications in all walks of life, including relationships, friendships, marriage, or business relationships. The house strongly influences your ability to cooperate with others, reach an understanding, make compromises, and work with another person toward whatever goal. This is the influence that makes a person diplomatic and amicable.

The seventh house has a special knack for partnerships that have the potential to change your life. The importance of planetary placements in this house is in how they might affect your ability to relate to other people and ensure that your partnerships are at the right balance between self-interest and sacrifice. With some luck, beneficial placements in the seventh house can help you be a better spouse, friend, or excel in business, particularly when deals are made, negotiations to be exercised, and contracts to be signed. The seventh house can also influence how you deal with your enemies and opponents in whatever area of life you encounter them.

The House of Transformation

- **Keywords:** Mergers, intimacy, sexuality, inheritance, investments, assets, property, joint efforts, death
- **Ruling Sign:** Scorpio
- **Planet:** Pluto

The eighth house goes by several names, including the house of transformation, sex, death, and debt. It's no accident that this house is the home of Scorpio, the most mysterious, reclusive, and cryptic of the zodiac signs. The house itself is somewhat mysterious, with peculiar energies flowing through and from it, influencing a few different areas of your life. Death and rebirth are important themes in this house, which can translate into profound personal changes and transformations over a lifetime – not just death and birth.

Depending on which planets venture through the eighth house at birth, the house could strongly influence the mystery. Depending on other astrological factors, this can manifest as a deep interest in the supernatural and the occult. The eighth house also involves sexuality, commitments of all sorts, and finances, especially investments. When it comes to money, the thing to keep in mind is that the eighth house is generally associated with other people's money more than with yours. Joint financial ventures that require a pooling of resources, for instance, might be affected. Because of its association with regeneration and transformation, this house can also determine how you deal with and heal from emotional and psychological trauma.

The House of Purpose

- **Keywords:** Travel, philosophy, spirituality, religion, ideals, higher education, learning, wisdom, ethics
- **Ruling Sign:** Sagittarius
- **Planet:** Jupiter

The ninth house is another known by a few different names, including the house of purpose, travel, and philosophy. In the broadest sense, one of this house's most important themes is how you experience, comprehend, and figure out the world. That's why philosophy, travel, learning, spirituality, and higher education are all important aspects of this house. This house exerts influences that can help you attain a stronger sense of purpose, especially through the realizations that come from the endeavors mentioned above. These goals and ideals are reflected in this house's residing sign of Sagittarius.

If the ninth house had to be summarized in a word, that word should probably be "exploration." Beyond travel and physical exploration in the world, the ninth house drives us to explore ourselves, our minds, and all intellectual pursuits that lead to personal growth. When strong planets with compatible energies, such as Jupiter, pass through the ninth house at birth, the influences above this house can get quite pronounced. This mixture of energies can lead individuals on a path toward committing their lives to philosophy, teaching, or organized religion. Such placements are often associated with priests and other religious or spiritual leaders.

The House of Enterprise

- **Keywords:** Reputation, career, ambition, goals, structure, masculinity, fathers, expertise
- **Ruling Sign:** Capricorn
- **Planet:** Saturn

The tenth house is regarded as the house of career, enterprise, and social status. Professional life and public standing, meaning reputation and image, are central themes in the tenth house. This house is the home of Capricorn, so it's no surprise that it also affects authority, ambition, and drive. The house of enterprise exerts influence on individual and collective human endeavors that have to do with authority, particularly in the areas of government and other structures that hold the world together.

The tenth house is also associated with various authority figures you'll encounter in life, including bosses, doctors, or people you look up to.

More than just affecting the success and failure of a particular career, the planetary placements in your tenth house at birth can influence what field and direction that career will be in. Since career paths and professional life are such important facets of human existence, the house of enterprise is regarded by many astrologers as one of the most important houses in the zodiac. Its influence can determine an entire life story, so paying heed to any potential placements that a birth chart might show you regarding this house is important. The tenth house's influence can also contribute to career changes and transformations at any point in life.

The House of Blessings

- **Keywords:** Friends, groups, humanism, hope, goals, wishes
- **Ruling Sign:** Aquarius
- **Planet:** Uranus

The eleventh house is the house of blessings, also known as the house of friendship. Similar to how the seventh house of partnerships affects one-on-one relationships, the eleventh house is about groups and how you interact with or fit in with them. Therefore, it makes perfect sense that the sociable and team-oriented Aquarius finds its home in this astrological domicile. However, this house's energy isn't just about personal networks and friendships. In a broader sense, it also governs things like humanitarian endeavors and our relations with society in general. The eleventh house can influence the degree to which you feel you belong in your wider environment, such as a culture or nation. This influence can also act as a guide that helps you identify your role in such a collective.

The eleventh house is also associated with fulfilling goals and wishes, which often translates into material gains and wealth. It's also marked by other relatively broad themes like love and happiness, particularly when it comes to how we share these joys with others.

The House of Sacrifice

- **Keywords**: Endings, seclusion, closure, healing, aging, afterlife, subtlety, escapism
- **Ruling Sign**: Pisces

- **Planet:** Neptune

The twelfth and final astrological house is often called the house of sacrifice, in keeping with its resident sign of Pisces. The ever-committed and sacrificial Pisces is right at home in this house. With certain planetary placements, the twelfth house's energy can turn Pisces folks into some of the finest people you could ever hope to meet.

Alternatively, the twelfth house is also called the house of the unconscious. Just as the unconscious is something that resides right under the surface, the twelfth house is the place that was located right on the horizon as you were being born. Just like the eighth house, this house is open to some interpretation and associated with various influences, some of which are pretty abstract. Dreams, emotions, intuition, and other unseen things that come from deep within are all influenced by the twelfth house. Intuitive and emotional energies such as those of the moon and Neptune can make this house and its energy an incredibly potent force in your life. Since Pisces are already known for their intuitive and reflective nature, these placements can make the Fish so invested in their inner world that they forget themselves.

Chapter 6: Major Planetary Aspects

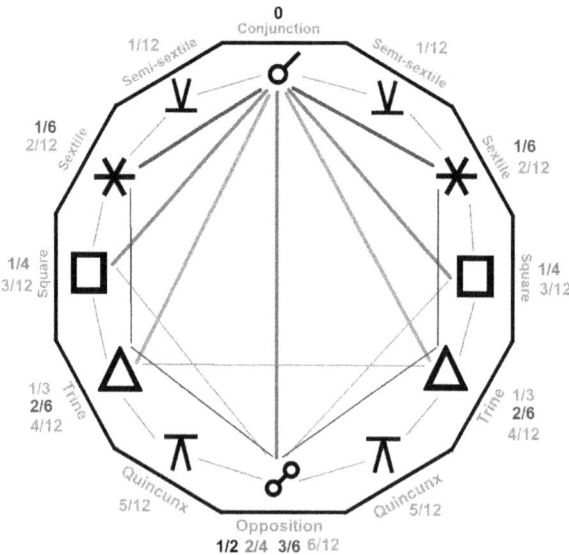

Major planetary aspects.

Tomruen, CC BY-SA 4.0 <https://creativecommons.org/licenses/by-sa/4.0>, via Wikimedia Commons https://commons.wikimedia.org/wiki/File:12_astrological_aspects.png

Planetary aspects, also known as astrological aspects, represent relationships between different planets in your chart. On your birth chart, these astrological aspects are represented by lines that can be seen connecting different planets on the chart. These aspects are generally divided into two categories, including major and minor planetary aspects. Among major planetary aspects, we have conjunction, sextile, square, trine, and opposition, all of which are defined by the angle at which two planets on a chart are connected at the center. Since the center of a chart represents the Earth, which is our point of view, planetary aspects are determined by drawing straight lines between planets and the center of the chart and then looking at the angle at which the lines from the two planets meet.

In the simplest terms, planetary aspects represent special relationships or partnerships, so to speak, between planets in your chart. This means that these planets will join their energies and traits for a specific astrological influence in your life. This can have several effects, which can be balancing, restraining, or energizing, depending on the aspect, the planets in question, and the signs that those planets occupy, among other things. The interaction between planets and zodiac signs is another important part of planetary aspects. In this chapter, we'll look closely at major planetary aspects, what each means, and how it affects you. While each aspect has a general interpretation and its associations, the effect of that aspect on you'll still ultimately depend on which planets are at play, thanks to their individual traits and energies.

Conjunction

The astrological conjunction of two planets occurs when those two planets are very close to each other, usually in the same zodiac sign, around the same degree. It's also possible for two planets to be close to each other but located on or near a cusp, which is essentially the line that separates consecutive zodiac signs or astrological houses in the zodiac wheel or horoscope. In practical terms, this means that two planets are very close to each other in the sky, as observed from the Earth, at the moment of your birth.

Strictly astrologically speaking, astrologers generally view conjunction as the strongest aspect. This aspect is essentially a tight bond between the two planets in question. That bond is characterized by creating a combination of the energies of these two planets, which feed into and affect each other in various ways. The results of this interaction will depend on several factors, including the traits of the planets, the sign they are positioned in, and their houses. Once the energies of two planets blend in conjunction, their inherent traits and associations can be amplified, inhibited, or modified in some other way. Some planets are more compatible than others, so it's important to be well-acquainted with all of them.

For example, if a person's chart shows that their sun and Venus are in conjunction, this can be quite a powerful and energizing influence. Nonetheless, the sign that this conjunction occurs can be a decisive factor. For a fiery and aggressive sign like Aries, Venus can act as a mitigating and loving influence that curtails Ram's aggressiveness with kindness and love. On the other hand, a conjunction between the sun and Mars can exacerbate the aggressive nature of Aries. Either way, this is a prime example of how the same aspect can influence two different people very differently, thanks to the unique properties of the planets. Lastly, one planet will usually dominate the other in conjunction, depending on the sign and house where the conjunction occurs. Conjunctions may also occur with more than two planets, a kind of conjunction referred to as stellium.

Because of these variations, conjunctions don't necessarily have to be "favorable," even though they usually are. According to most astrologers, energies like those of Venus and Jupiter are generally desirable and beneficial in conjunctions. Planets like Mars or Saturn, on the other hand, are generally disruptive and tend to not get along very well with most planets in conjunction. This doesn't mean that such conjunctions are a curse that will doom you to suffer. These conjunctions are just a potential challenge, and, as such, they serve their purpose in your life, such as by making you stronger and enticing you to grow as a person.

Sextile

When planets are located 60 degrees or two signs apart on the chart, they are in what's called a sextile aspect. Astrologers consider this aspect of being highly positive, with the planets in question supporting each other while also fostering a mutually beneficial relationship between the zodiac signs they occupy. Sextiles are thus harmonious partnerships that allow signs to complement each other, which can manifest in several favorable ways, depending on the unique characteristics of your chart. All signs and planets generally have positive sides and traits, which a sextile aspect allows to blossom and come to the forefront. Technically speaking, the sextile is a harmonious and complementary aspect because planets that occupy chart positions 60 degrees apart will always fall into zodiac signs that are elementally complementary, meaning earth and water or fire and air.

This aspect isn't always as strong and active as some other aspects, but it's important, nonetheless. Frequently, a sextile can give one of your planets just the boost it needs to provide a more positive influence in your life. For instance, if you get Mars in a sextile with one of the planets in your chart, that planet can benefit from the aggressive and courageous nature of Mars, helping you balance out another planet's weaknesses. A sextile is an astrological aspect with no losers or drawbacks. It never poses challenges or makes planets weaker; it just ensures you get the best of everything.

The sextile aspect is also referred to as a halved trine, a similar but more powerful aspect. If this aspect were to be described in a few keywords, they would include things like "excitement," "support," "simple," and "comfortable." One of the best characteristics of this harmonious aspect is that it allows a free flow of ideas and inspiration between signs. It's not uncommon for sextiles to bolster people's creative, artistic side, helping them express what's inside. Sextiles are also associated with gifts, talents, and skills that we already have. Since many take these things for granted instead of using them to their full extent, a sextile in your chart can help energize you to further sharpen your talents and work on yourself. The flow of information, communication, relaxation, and camaraderie are some themes connected to sextiles.

Square

When planets are separated by around 90 degrees, they are in a square aspect. Right off the bat, a chart containing a square aspect shows us that the planets with this aspect are in signs of incompatible elements but the same modality. Their signs will also occupy different quadrants. These are some of the factors that make squares into powerful astrological aspects and produce some tension between the planets and the signs they occupy. As an intense aspect, the square is easily and visibly manifested, exerting substantial influence.

The tension, as mentioned above, isn't necessarily a bad thing, though. This tension can show you where and how you need to improve, and the pressure can often be just the thing you need to jump into action. Even though astrologers consider this to be the most difficult astrological aspect, you shouldn't shy away from what it can tell you in your birth chart. The tension and the difficulty of squares are in the collision of planetary energies. As usual, the key is to read into the specific planets and what they bring to the table so that you can see how exactly the planets are communicating under the umbrella of the square aspect.

Just as a sextile allows planets to show their brightest, most positive sides, a square does the opposite. This is when every planet's darker, shadowy side comes out and is then faced head-on with the same side of the other planet. Naturally, this results in a powerful clash of energies, resulting in frustration and conflict. As the planets struggle to outperform each other, the more dominant influence will generally prevail and determine most of the characteristics of this astrological aspect.

Just as planets with this aspect show their shadowy sides, so do squares help us identify similar sides of ourselves. This can mean flaws but also wounds that we need to heal, and a square aspect in your chart can be a useful pointer in that direction. It's important to remember that each challenge yields a reward, which is why square aspects are something you should work with instead of shunning them. Compromise is always a good way to deal with the conflict and tension at work here.

Trine

A trine aspect is similar to a sextile, but this aspect tends to be more potent and intense as an astrological influence. This is also a positive aspect with generally favorable energy, and it occurs when planets are apart by around 120 degrees, which amounts to four zodiac signs on the wheel. The signs that planets in trine fall on will always have the same element, naturally producing agreement and synergy. This aspect is often associated with good luck, peace, and new opportunities. This energy reveals new paths to us and energizes us to move forward and make progress in life on whatever front is important.

As with sextiles, the issue with trines is that they are so comfortable, which is why it's so easy to go the lazy route and neglect what a trine might be telling you. Square aspects keep you on your toes through their tension and conflict, pushing you to take action out of necessity and discomfort, whereas your planets in trine will require some personal initiative. Still, this is just a minor drawback that's easily manageable. In general, trines are one of the most desirable aspects and, in many ways, they are even better than sextiles.

As always, consider the different energies that planets in this aspect might bring. If Venus brings love and creativity to the table, then a trine aspect with Jupiter, which tends to bring good luck, can produce very favorable influences in the areas of love and art. A particularly powerful placement can occur when three planets happen to form a triangle on your birth chart, each occupying a sign with the same element. This aspect is known as the grand trine and will ensure the free flow of all the best characteristics and energies of the three planets in question. This powerful combination can bless you with many gifts and a whole lot of good fortune, all of which will manifest differently depending on the planets forming the grand trine. At the same time, it's important to remember that such domination of trines in your birth chart can make things so comfortable that your motivation to self-improve can wane, which is something to look out for.

Opposition

As its name suggests, *opposition* is an aspect in which two planets occupy positions opposite each other in the sky at around 180 degrees or six zodiac signs apart. Polarity and conflict are the central themes of this aspect, which is all about balance and learning how to maintain it. If you approach this aspect correctly, though, it can be of great help and teach you many lessons. As such, this aspect is a potentially difficult and tense one, but it's generally more favorable than square.

An opposition aspect in the birth chart can manifest as a pronounced duality in some people. Think of mood swings, alternations between extremes of any kind, and an overall inclination toward rapid changes. The opposition aspect has one significant mitigating factor: the compatibility of elements of the signs that the planets occupy. This compatibility is often the key to getting a grip on an opposition aspect in the chart and getting it under control.

The opposing signs and their occupying planets can find a common tongue and eventually start working in unison through compromise. Of course, this heavily depends on the planets in the equation and how their energies interact. Even though two planets can fall into opposition, their traits can be quite complementary, fitting together as two opposite pieces into one functional whole. The elemental compatibility plays a major role in this regard, but the greatest factor will be your personal effort to make these influences work together. The fact that the opposing signs will share their modality is another problem that can make understanding difficult, but if you try hard enough, compromises are possible.

You must interpret the planets in your chart, analyze their traits, and see how this information relates to your life. The opposite planets can show you which flaws you need to work on, which fronts to push, and where to take a more relaxed approach. This is how the conflicting influences of opposing planets can be balanced out, ultimately helping you get the best out of this compromise. It's also important to consider which of the planets is more dominant since it's likely that this will be the one you have to work with.

Chapter 7: Minor Planetary Aspects

Although major planetary aspects are usually considered to be the most important or "main" aspects, so to speak, there are also minor planetary aspects. The aspects in this category are more numerous, and they can exert various astrological influences on a person's birth chart. Consequently, these aspects can be very important for an accurate reading of your chart and for just getting more out of practical astrology, in general.

Some minor aspects are more frequently mentioned and analyzed than others, but the more you learn about them, the more tools you'll have available. Generally speaking, minor aspects are associated with some of your chart's subtle influences and forces. Some astrologers describe minor aspects as related to all things "magical." They are also more open to interpretation, with less fixed meanings than those of major aspects. The fact that their influence is rarely completely clear is one of the reasons why these aspects are associated with the magical and the occult.

Some astrologers will classify minor astrological aspects into two categories; one has to do with special abilities and the other with karmic forces. These two categories also have their mantras: "I do" and "I did," respectively. Because the number of minor aspects can get quite high, astrologers generally limit their number to a few more commonly interpreted aspects depending on how deep we delve into a chart. They are also further divided into proper and rare minor aspects. It's important not to let the word "minor" fool you, as these aspects can be just as important as major ones and will often provide the exact bit of information you need to reach a valuable conclusion when reading a chart. In this chapter, we'll look at ten minor aspects that tend to show up in charts most frequently.

Semi-Sextile

As you may have gathered from its name, the semi-sextile aspect occurs when planets are positioned with a 30-degree separation or one-half of a sextile. This means the planets will be located in two consecutive or neighboring zodiac signs for the planetary placement. This has a few implications in the astrological sense, one of which is that the two planets have no line of sight between them. As such, semi-sextile aspects produce some tension and uncertainty, but they are ultimately manageable.

The planets in this aspect will have a degree of attraction between them by virtue of their closeness alone. Still, it might take some effort to make the two planets' energies and influences come together as they should. As with most other problematic astrological aspects, compromise is the best course toward that end. Consecutive signs in the zodiac are always very different from each other, diverging in modality, polarity, and element. Add to that the potential conflict between the energies of two very different planets occupying those signs, and you have a problematic mix that needs sorting out.

Being a minor aspect, semi-sextile isn't the most influential aspect you can find in a birth chart, but it's worth noting for its association with potential. When looking at the traits and energies that the planets in question bring to the table, these factors can be read as influences that might or might not be at work. If your particular chart implies that your semi-sextile planets could do you some good, this is certainly worth exploring.

Quincunx

The quincunx aspect, also known as the *inconjunct aspect*, occurs when planets are positioned around 150 degrees apart on the chart. *Inconjunction* is another aspect that brings some tension and unease to the table. Even so, this is the aspect that most astrologers consider to be the most important among the minor aspects. Planets in this aspect conflict, and their energies will usually be in a perpetual state of conflict, with the dominant planet exerting stronger influence and suppressing the other.

This is another one of those aspects where the analysis of your chart and some introspection can help you figure out the best way to balance conflicting astrological influences. Depending on the planets and signs in question, which can certainly be difficult, but the self-realization and improvement that might come as a result will be worth the effort. Quincunx can be surprisingly influential and noticeable in your life for a minor astrological aspect.

If you often feel frustrated, torn between different options and sources of pressure, or just conflicted, you might have a quincunx aspect in your chart. If quincunx had to be described in a word, that would be stress. You can view this aspect as two individual energies that have nothing in common and are at odds of being locked together in a small room. This is exactly what's happening with planets in inconjunction, a disturbance that requires work. The quincunx aspect is also associated with karma and medicine.

Quintile

Semi-sextile and quincunx are generally considered the two main aspects within the minor category. The numerous other minor astrological aspects are usually classified as less important, but they can undoubtedly exert a noticeable influence on your life. When all those other details of your birth chart are just not enough, and some questions still remain unanswered, it will be time to dig deeper, and that's where additional astrological aspects come into play, no matter how unimportant they might seem to some.

One of these less common aspects is the quintile aspect, which occurs when planets are around 72 degrees apart from each other. The quintile aspect is generally a positive and favorable influence, mostly associated with innate talents and delicate senses. This aspect can be quite energizing, fueling things like ambition and the desire for self-expression. Riding the wave of this aspect, you may also feel a heightened drive to impact the world. The keen and heightened senses that this aspect nurtures can also allow you to see things beyond the surface level, gaining insights that most other people might miss.

Still, quintile isn't the kind of aspect that will do things for you, as it will require you to make an effort to tap into your talents and intuition.

Quintile is a harmonious aspect, and it divides the wheel into five equal parts while also forming a five-point star in the chart. Even though astrologers often overlook this aspect, it's been known to unveil lessons and potential that would otherwise remain hidden.

Bi-Quintile

Planets are in a bi-quintile aspect when they are separated by around 144 degrees on the chart. Like the quintile aspect, the bi-quintile aspect is a favorable aspect with positive influences, although astrologers generally neglect it. A bi-quintile aspect amounts to two quintiles or, more precisely, one-third of the chart's circle. Depending on planetary placements, a birth chart can contain more than one bi-quintile aspect. When two of them are joined together, their lines form a shape resembling the tip of a spear or arrow, which is a powerful influence as far as minor aspects go.

Just as the quintile aspect falls between sextile and square, representing talent and creativity crises, the bi-quintile aspect is situated between the discomfort of the sesquiquadrate and the need to adjust, which is associated with quincunx. All this means is that the bi-quintile aspect is strongly associated with artistic pursuits, which is even more pronounced than in the quintile aspect. This aspect also urges the individual to be even more expressive and to share their ideas with the world. Remember that both quintile and bi-quintile aspects can shed light on hidden talents if you know where to look. If you're wondering what you're good at and whether you have a knack for certain skills, make sure you find out whether some of these aspects are at work somewhere in your birth chart.

Septile

Under the septile aspects, there are regular septile, bi-septile, and tri-septile ones, which start with the basic septile that divides planets by 51 degrees and 25 minutes on the chart. The base septile divides the horoscope into seven equal parts and is considered to be one of the rarer aspects that might show up in a birth chart.

The septile aspect has some powerful associations with symbolism, including the heptagram and the number seven. The heptagram (seven-point star) relates to the broader sense of the seven planetary spheres and time passage. Astrologers also associate this aspect with divinity and spirituality, which is clearly symbolized by the number seven. This number has long had a lot of symbolic power in religion, with very strong spiritual connotations. The septile can thus be a very inspiring aspect that tends to foster the human sense of wonder and our awe of the universe in all its greatness. This kind of influence nurtures spiritual growth and can help you on your path toward a higher awareness and state of mind, whether concerning spirituality, art, or some other endeavor that comes from within.

This aspect of deeper insight and vision stretches beyond just the individual and their earthly concerns. To harness the energy of a septile aspect, assuming that it occurs in your chart, is to tune into dimensions beyond our basic comprehension.

Octile

The octile aspect occurs between planets 45 degrees apart on the chart. Since this is half of a 90-degree angle, it is also called the semi-square aspect. The octile aspect is the eighth part of the full chart circle and is in many ways a smaller-scale version of the square aspect. This means that it retains many of the square aspect's adverse effects like tension, stress, and conflict, but with lower intensity.

Like the square aspect, octile can help you pinpoint certain problem areas and present challenges you need to surmount to enact meaningful action and make changes in your life where needed. Restlessness, discomfort, and subtle annoyance can be symptoms of the influence of an octile aspect that must be addressed. Like squares, this adverse planetary aspect represents an opportunity just as much as a nuisance. The fact that the semi-square aspect is less intense than the full square also has a flip side.

While its influence may be weaker, this also means that it can be more difficult to feel and detect, which can cause difficulties in identifying the problem. This makes the tension and the conflict in the chart very easy to ignore and sweep under the rug. As tempting as this might be to most people, it's a bad idea to leave this tension unchecked. There are also semi-octiles, which divide the chart into parts that are half the size of those made by regular octiles, meaning 22.5 degrees. This aspect is even rarer and less frequently used than octile.

Sesquiquadrate

Also called the *sesquisquare* or *trioctile aspect*, this peculiarly named planetary aspect occurs when planets are placed 135 degrees apart from each other. This is another one among the conflicted aspects as the planets that have it won't be inclined to interact in a productive, constructive manner. As is always the case in such astrological arrangements, tension is bound to emerge. You might have to address another conflict, assuming that this rare aspect shows up in your chart.

As always, when dealing with such aspects, this conflict should be resolved through compromise. As long as you can focus on adopting the best of both planets, you should be able to balance this minor aspect. Getting on good terms with the trioctile aspect is easier through honesty, particularly honesty with yourself. A lot of this aspect's tension also comes from the fact that it amounts to a square and a half. This aspect can form an octagram on a horoscope consisting of two squares imposed over each other. This is why some astrologers interpret the sesquiquadrate aspect as the "super square." The intensity of this aspect is only mitigated by its rareness and its being a minor aspect.

The conflicts that the sesquiquadrate aspect is associated with have a lot to do with karma as well. This is why this aspect is sometimes referred to as the karmic key of the birth chart. Conflicting values and inner turmoil over tough moral questions are common themes. Because of the subtle nature of minor aspects, this conflict often goes on in the subconscious mind, where it can easily go unnoticed. Becoming aware of this conflict will help you mend such turmoil, which is how a sesquiquadrate can be used to your advantage when it occurs in your chart.

Novile

Novile aspects are also called *noniles* or *nonagons*, which occur when planets are 40 degrees apart. This minor, often-overlooked aspect has a very specific association with pregnancy and the whole creation process, and some astrologers refer to it as the aspect of completion. This influence can apply to numerous areas of life and its experiences beyond actual pregnancy. The inception, birth, and growth of ideas, for instance, are common themes associated with the novile aspect.

Furthermore, the association with birth also carries over into the topic of transformation. A novile aspect in your chart can often point to the end of some sort of phase or ongoing process that may have been taking place in your life for a while. On the flip side, it can also symbolize the beginning of something new. In either case, this subtle astrological aspect will exert energies only the most sensitive individuals will pick up on. Still, this is undoubtedly a helpful aspect worth paying attention to when identified. Novile aspects can also come in the form of bi-novile and quadra-novile if suitable planetary placements occur in a birth chart.

Decile and Undecile

Planets possess a *decile* aspect when they are 36 degrees apart on your chart. The decile aspect thus cuts the chart into ten equal parts. In general, decile is viewed as favorable with some benefits, even though its effect is diminished by being a minor and rare aspect. Like some of the aspects above, the decile aspect has a lot to do with all things hidden, especially talents that lie dormant in the individual and are untapped. Whereas an aspect like quintile is associated with strong and already considerably honed talents, decile energizes talents that you may be completely unaware of. It's an aspect of hidden gifts yet waiting to be harvested.

There are also trideciles and quindeciles, separating the planets by 108 and 24 degrees, respectively. The quindecile aspect is referred to by some astrologers as "the fatal in the natal," and it can refer to obsessions and all things involuntary and compulsive. When present and felt, this aspect can somewhat detach the individual from reality, at least regarding the traits and areas of life governed by the planets in quindecile on the chart.

The *undecile* aspect occurs when planets are 32 degrees and 44 minutes apart. This is the eleventh part of the chart, making for a much less rounded division of the chart than decile. Like some of the other aspects we've covered, this aspect is a relatively recent addition to astrology and wasn't used traditionally. Nowadays, it's mostly used in the astrological practice known as *Harmonics*. Apart from the regular undecile aspect, there are also biundecile, triundecile, quadraundecile, and quintundecile aspects.

Chapter 8: Interpreting Natal Charts

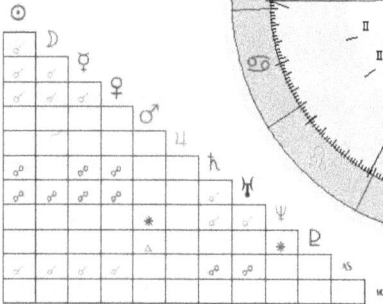

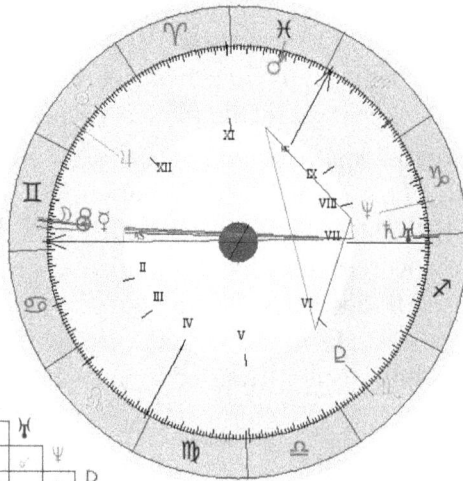

Sample birth chart.

No machine-readable author provided. Leopanza~commonswiki assumed (based on copyright claims)., CC BY-SA 3.0 <http://creativecommons.org/licenses/by-sa/3.0/>, via Wikimedia Commons https://commons.wikimedia.org/wiki/File:Birth_chart_example.JPG

Once you get a handle on the basics of practical astrology, the only thing that remains is to apply all of that theoretical knowledge in practice and start reading your stars. As mentioned before, whether online or in-

---

person, astrologers can help you put together a birth chart and interpret it, but this doesn't mean you shouldn't learn how to do it yourself. With various online tools at your disposal, making your own birth chart has never been easier, so all you need to get started is to know what you're looking at.

As you've seen in this book thus far, there is quite a lot to unpack when practicing astrology. Astrology is an intricate network of interwoven factors that all feed into each other and interact in many different ways. You and your life are caught up right in the middle of this storm of energies that permeate the skies above. Since you know how to read and interpret the basic astrological factors individually, we'll take a chapter to explore the aforementioned birth charts and how you can start reading yours.

What Is a Birth Chart?

You've noticed that we've made many mentions of birth charts by now, and that's with good reason. All of that other theoretical knowledge inevitably leads to the art of chart reading. As we've indicated by now, your birth chart can be seen as a symbolic representation of your personality since it's essentially a snapshot of the visible sky at the moment of your birth. For this reason, creating a chart requires not just the day, month, and year but also the place and exact time of your birth.

The birth or natal chart is also known by other names, including astrological chart, celestial map, cosmogram, radix, chart wheel, or just *chart*. You'll often see the term "horoscope" used interchangeably with birth charts. The chances are that you've already seen a birth chart or two, at least in passing, as they have a very distinct look. The chart consists of a wheel or circle with multiple layers divided into various equal parts, depending on what that layer represents. A typical chart template includes zodiac signs, degree markings, houses, and a central circle.

The division of the ecliptic plane into twelve houses may or may not consist of twelve equal parts of 30 degrees each, depending on the system being used. The position of the first house depends on the information the chart is based on, but the cusp (the line between two houses or signs) of the first house will always begin at the ascendant. This first house determines the rest of the houses, which follow counterclockwise around the wheel. As we've already mentioned in passing, the ascendant represents the exact point rising just over the eastern horizon at your birth, so it clearly depends on the Earth's rotation. This is an incredibly important factor that determines your birth chart and is crucial for interpreting it.

You'll also notice that the central circle often contains numerous lines connecting various points in the circle, with many lines being off-center. The lines are often in different colors because they need to be differentiated to represent aspects. That's more or less a basic description of what a birth chart looks like, but there can be some variations, depending on the methodology of the astrologer.

In terms of history, it took a while from those early days of ancient astrology until astrologers began to use what we might consider birth charts in the contemporary sense. Still, the practice of making and reading birth charts is quite old, even if not as old as astrology itself. Some of the earliest recognizable birth charts or horoscopes date back to around 400 BC.

Apart from regular natal charts, many astrological charts follow similar principles and are used to get a reading of other things that might interest an astrologer. One example is the so-called compatibility chart, which aims to show how well you would get along with others. Compatibility charts are generally divided into synastry charts, which compare the planets in two natal charts, and composite charts, which blend two given charts into one, focusing on the relationship potential between the two.

Another example of an astrological chart is the solar return chart, which is a yearly chart that analyzes the period between two birthdays. There are also astrological charts that focus exclusively on helping you plan events. Getting an event chart is simply the matter of creating a chart based on the event's date, time, and location. Remember, birth charts are also event charts, with the event in focus being a person's birth, so the methodology can work with most other events just as well. If you have an important upcoming interview or are pondering when you should schedule a big celebration of some sort, reading an astrological chart can help you get some idea about the astrological circumstances and overall fortune you can expect.

Astrological charts have also seen some variations among different cultures. Apart from Western astrology, Vedic and Chinese astrological practices have also produced charts and similar methods to perform astrological readings. Some calculations and underlying principles will differ from those in the West, but the overall objective remains the same. One of the most prominent differences in China is the Chinese zodiac with its fairly famous system of animals, elements, and years.

Reading What's Written

Throughout our previous chapters, you've already learned much of the fundamental knowledge you need to read a natal chart. Understanding all those factors at play will get you more than halfway toward becoming a chart reader, but you'll still have to learn a few more things. With the theoretical side of things taken care of, the next order of business is to familiarize yourself with the visual aspects of a birth chart.

When you look at any chart, you'll see that it's essentially a circle filled with all sorts of symbols, lines, and other visual representations of the astrological factors at work. These symbols are the written language of astrology, and you'll have to get a handle on them if you are to read charts, but this won't take too much effort. The symbols will help you read, and the theoretical knowledge we've covered thus far will help you interpret, and that's pretty much what birth chart reading boils down to.

The first practical step toward reading your chart is to make one. This is very easy to do nowadays, thanks to online resources that will automatically make a chart for you based on inputted information. A simple Internet search will reveal many websites that offer this tool. Simply put in the time, date, and place of your birth, and the algorithm will do the rest for you. In case you don't know and can't find out the exact time of your birth, most algorithms will ask you to name noon as the time of birth. This will make the chart somewhat less accurate, but there'll still be more than plenty of stuff for you to analyze.

If you're a beginner, it's a good idea to get yourself a sheet or legend of astrological symbols to keep handy because it will take a bit of practice and time until you've mastered the written language of astrology. Once you pull up your birth chart, it's time to apply what you've learned about the traits and energies of planets, zodiac signs, astrological houses, and aspects, which will be more than enough for a basic but solid reading.

Reading the symbols, one of the first things you'll notice is that the planets occupy specific points on the wheel in a very unique and uneven order throughout the twelve signs. This is the essence of your chart and will account for much of the information you will read. The first thing to note is your own sun sign, which you've probably known all your life. Take note of which planets are inside of that sign or close to it, and then you can begin interpreting the influences at play.

Remember that many of the algorithms and tools on the Internet will also provide you with their own interpretations of your birth chart. However, you might not want to rely on these automated readings because their scope is limited, and the information will usually be very simplistic, often lacking context. If you just get a robotic list of traits, predictions, and assumptions without a cohesive and coherent narrative, you might baselessly arrive at some negative or demoralizing conclusions. The best thing to do is to use your own knowledge and become better at interpreting through practice or talking to a professional astrologer.

Beyond your sun sign, look closely at all the other planetary placements and use this book for reference to determine what those placements mean. Remember, even if you see certain less than favorable placements, there are still aspects, astrological houses, and other factors that often mitigate negative effects or create unique synergies of influences that you might miss if you focus on your placements. When analyzing the placements, it's also important to remember your sign's ruling planet to see how it fares on your chart.

A good way to read a chart is by having a few key goals or areas of interest, such as love or work. For instance, if you want to know what your prospects in life look like regarding love and relationships, pay special attention to intense planets and houses associated with these themes. When you know what you're looking for, chart reading becomes simpler and more focused, which will help you avoid getting bogged down in details that don't matter much to you.

Look out for rare phenomena such as stelliums, which we briefly mentioned earlier when discussing aspects. Three or more planets in a single sign are a powerful energy source, for better or worse. You should also pay attention to the balance of elements and modalities in your chart. All of these things are unique to your chart and are subject to so much variation that it's impossible to predict what you'll find when you delve into it. The best way to become an adept chart reader is just to get started. Make yourself a chart online, open this book, get a cup of coffee, and take your time studying this intricate puzzle.

Extra Tips

Sometimes, reading your charts can be particularly useful, particularly at the start of the year and on your birthday. The start of a new year is the perfect time to make a transit chart and look at what the planets might have in store for you. We'll take a closer look at planetary transits in our next chapter, but suffice it to say that transit charts are probably the most valuable astrological tool for forecasting the future. The analysis of transits often involves comparisons with your birth chart.

This is usually done by adding one more outer circle layer to a birth chart, which will contain the planetary symbols indicating where the planets are on that particular day. This way, astrologers can easily compare the positions between that day and the fixed positions of the planets in your natal chart. Needless to say, these would be some pretty advanced astrological readings, so it's normal if such a complex chart overwhelms you at first before you get your bearings.

Assuming you're a beginner at reading charts, you may want to start by following a certain order when looking at your chart. After looking at your sun sign, you can see what's going on with your moon and ascendant signs. Simply look for the moon symbol in your generated birth chart and note which sign it occupies. As for the ascendant, keep in mind that you'll only be able to determine it accurately if you've fed your exact time of birth into the chart calculation. Look at where the first house on your chart begins to determine your ascendant sign.

A good way to practice and get better at reading natal charts is to do a chart for someone else, particularly someone you know very well. Most people have some difficulty being objective and impartial about themselves, their traits, personality, flaws, and virtues, so you might initially find it a bit tough to see all those subtle connections between your life and your astrological influences. For some people, it's best to start by making their first chart about a close friend or family member as an introduction to the practice. Once you get the hang of it, you'll likely end up shocked at how many overlaps there are between what's on the chart and what you've seen in life.

Last but not least, it's worth pointing out certain patterns to look for when analyzing birth charts. This sort of thing will come more naturally after some practice, but there are ways to speed up your acclimation. One method you can apply is hemisphere analysis, which boils down to dividing the chart wheel in half horizontally and vertically and counting the number of planets on each side of the line. Another approach is pattern analysis, which focuses on how the planets are scattered around the wheel.

Both of these chart reading methods are set apart from traditional interpretation because they focus solely on the pattern of the planets in the chart as a source of information instead of interpreting the traits, energies, aspects, and everything else. As an example, if a hemisphere analysis shows you that there are seven planets above the horizontal line, this indicates that you are likely an extrovert. In the opposite case, you're probably an introvert. Conversely, the number of planets on either side of the vertical line measures the prevalence of dependence or independence in your personality.

This is only a tiny glance into another way of looking at birth charts. Since pattern analysis mostly circumvents detailed interpretation based on the theoretical knowledge we've covered, it's definitely worth looking into if you're a beginner. Simplicity means less accuracy, so keep in mind that detailed interpretation will be necessary for more accurate readings.

Chapter 9: Planetary Transits

Planetary transits are a somewhat overlooked aspect of practical astrology. While natal charts focus primarily on personal traits, helping you learn things about yourself and self-reflect, planetary transits are one of the tools used in an attempt to gain some insights into the future. Of course, the future is a fickle thing, so it's difficult to talk about it without engaging in conjecture. Planetary transits are useful because they provide a semblance of something concrete that can be analyzed and read to reach certain conclusions in this otherwise mysterious part of astrology.

While the term "planetary transit" seems to imply a generalized topic regarding the movement of celestial bodies, it actually refers to something more specific. In the simplest terms, a planetary transit is a move that a planet makes across your natal planets, which are the positions of planets in your natal chart. For example, consider a natal chart showing Mars in Aries at the time of your birth. A transit happens in the present time if a planet finds itself traversing across Aries and aligns with the point that Mars occupied in that sign at your birth. That alignment should be within 10 degrees at most to make the transit meaningful. As this happens, the planet in question is "transiting through your natal Mars," as astrologers would call the process. Another way to look at transits would be as aspects between a transiting planet and a planetary placement on your chart. Transiting aspects are defined by no more than a couple of degrees in deviation on either side of your natal planet.

Reading your transits is different than reading a natal chart in that your chart resembles a mere snapshot of the sky at the moment when you were born. As you've seen, your birth chart is a personal analysis that can help you better understand your strengths, weaknesses, feelings, and mentality. With transits, you'll look at where the planets are going, not just where they were positioned at a given moment. Since transits are occurrences that come and go, they often influence us in new, unexpected ways. Some common ways these effects manifest include substantial shifts of mood or feelings and other similar changes that come suddenly. These things happen because planets that are transiting through your natal planet bring energies that you're not used to.

As is often the case when astrological influences meet and interact, transits usually resemble a convergence of energies that blend together to produce certain results. Think about how a planet of communication such as Mercury might affect you if it transits through your natal Venus. Since Venus is a planet of love and Mercury governs communication and expression, you might find yourself more willing and comfortable to express your love to the people in your life who matter, such as family or friends. If Mars passes through natal Mercury, as another example, you may find yourself being more aggressive and open in how you communicate, for better or worse.

These are just two examples of the more specific effects transits can produce, but they don't always manifest. Sometimes, these energies will come into your life as a more subtle, general change in themes such as feelings, attitude, or mood. This influence can affect your daily life, but the intensity of the effects will vary based on many factors. Transits occurring through your natal sun or moon tend to produce these general, broader effects, while other planets will usually show more character according to their traits. The planetary rulership of your zodiac sign will also play a part.

Apart from influencing your inner world, the energies that come from planetary transits will also change how you radiate your energies and how they relate to the world. For example, a shift might occur in the type of people you attract and run into. Attraction goes beyond just people, too, meaning that planetary transits might affect the kind of luck and fortune you attract. In general, if you want to better understand how the planets affect you beyond just the basics, then transits are something you should read into. The upcoming movements of all the celestial bodies in our sky can be astronomically predicted, so there's always plenty to learn about what's coming.

Planetary transits are generally classified into the outer and inner categories, defined by the distance of our solar system's planets from the sun. This chapter will take a closer look at both of these categories and some of the characteristics of how each of the main planets behaves and interacts when transiting through signs and houses.

Outer Transits

The outer planets are typically what astrologers analyze first when getting a reading of your planetary transits. As you might remember from what we discussed about the individual planets and their characteristics earlier, some planets take a very long time to traverse the zodiac. This is because the distant planets have a much longer journey around the sun. As such, some of the furthest planets like Neptune and Pluto will take centuries to make transits, which makes for some very rare astrological events.

Because the outer planets take longer to make their transits, astrologers tend to focus primarily on them when trying to get a read on what lies ahead. This is because these planets allow sufficient time for planning and thinking in advance. The planets whose transits fall into the outer category include Jupiter, Saturn, Uranus, Neptune, and Pluto.

Jupiter

Jupiter in transit is a powerful influence, especially regarding its energy of expansion and enlargement. Jupiter's transit takes months, so it has the potential to affect a considerable period in your life and help you get a lot done. This transit is also a time of opportunity, particularly in those areas of your life affected by the natal planet Jupiter is transiting through. This transit tends to bring a lot of good luck, especially in all things related to business and your professional life in general. Jupiter's transit can be a time of all manner of novelty. Depending on the aspects, this transit can bring some negative influences, too, leading to errors in judgment, loss of control, or a streak of bad luck.

Saturn

On the other hand, Saturn's transit can spell a whole lot of trouble for people. The intensity of transiting Saturn's effects will vary depending on which planet it passes through. Still, some common themes to be expected include restriction, diminishing energy levels, mood swings, potential health issues, miscommunication, losses of all sorts, and overall bad luck. Because this transit affects communication, you may also experience some setbacks in your social standing and respect. Nonetheless, Saturn's transit will afford you some opportunities to lay low, consolidate, self-improve, and plan for the long term. Patience and restraint are the names of the game during this transit, and if you play it right, the transit will amount to little more than a temporary slowdown in your life. And if you try, it might even end up as beneficial for you, thanks to lessons learned and preparations made before you get back on top of things after the transit.

Uranus

The transit of Uranus can be kind of dramatic at times. This planet tends to stir up quite a commotion when transiting, leading to major changes and turnovers. This can be good or bad, depending on the natal planet and on how you handle this period. It's an opportunity to make major life changes and start going in completely new directions. Just as it can cause upheaval in your life, so it can affect your mind and character, making you feel rebellious or unusually creative and inspired. It's a time of unconventional ideas and originality for you as the transit stokes the fires of your individuality and sense of freedom.

Neptune

Neptune can bring in quite a bit of mystery and confusion, making its transit a period of unclear, strange, and downright peculiar circumstances. This isn't necessarily bad, as this transit's peculiar energy also fosters your creativity and inspiration. When Neptune forms an aspect with a natal planet or an astrological house in your chart, it has a tendency to make their associated ideas and feelings less clear. This can make you prone to ideological thinking, which can be either positive or negative, depending on the context. The transit of Neptune has considerable spiritual implications, too, making this a good time to focus on the spiritual or religious side of your life. Because of this, this transit can be highly beneficial, as long as you don't veer off into escapism or overthinking to the point of delusion. It's also a time to be wary of addiction and substance abuse.

Pluto

As you can probably predict from what you learned about the planets earlier, Pluto's transit is often a time of massive changes and transformations, with personal and general implications. This is when old stories end and new ones commence, usually after having subtly developed under the surface for some time before that point. Pluto's transformative energy will also affect the themes, ideas, and traits of the natal planet or house with which the transit forms an aspect. Pluto's transit also has the potential to rekindle the flames of old problems that you may have thought were buried, forcing you to deal with past baggage.

Inner Transits

Most astrologers give less importance to inner transits than outer ones, and the main reason for this is that inner transits pass so quickly. Their quick passing gives them a very limited window to exert transitory energies and influence, severely constraining their power in this regard. Nonetheless, the transits of each of these planets do have certain characteristics and effects, which the most committed astrologers will occasionally take into account. The inner planets include the sun, the moon, Mercury, Venus, and Mars.

The Sun

The sun's transit is a relatively short affair, exerting the maximum of its influence for around two days at a time. This transit can have various effects depending on the natal planet, sign, or house that the sun is transiting through. In general, physical and mental health are very common areas that the sun affects. As you know, the sun is a highly energizing and radiant planet in astrology, so its transit also has the potential to make you more active, outgoing, expressive, and creative. The sun in transit can also affect your willpower, usually beneficially, but this will depend on the aspect.

The Moon

The moon has a very fast transit, usually lasting only for a few hours. The effects of the moon on people have long been the object of speculation and theories, and astrological transits are certainly part of that picture. When the moon is in transit, it will mostly influence your mood and emotional state, as its planetary traits already suggest. The energy radiated by the moon in transit is usually not very intense, though, so its effects can be quite subtle and subconscious. The effect will usually be modified by the natal planet, house, or sign in question. Planets that affect emotions, such as Neptune, can produce noticeable results when combined with the moon.

Mercury

Being the closest planet to the sun, Mercury gets through the zodiac pretty quickly, with its peak transit usually lasting for a couple of days at most. The effects of Mercury's transit are mostly in line with the planet's traits, particularly its governance over communication. This is a good time to communicate with people, have important conversations, write to your friends, or rekindle old friendships with a sudden visit. Depending on what aspects Mercury forms in transit, it can affect your thinking for better or worse. Mercury's transit can also be a good opportunity for making a minor journey or some small positive change in life.

Venus

The transit of Venus lasts about the same as Mercury's, peaking for a couple of days at most. Venus' themes of love and beauty are significant factors in this transit, meaning that it can be a time of strong feelings, especially good ones. Since we express love in several ways, including through material sharing, the transit of Venus can sometimes bring about gifts and presents. Those couple of days can be an especially good time for romance if Venus transits through natal Uranus. Venus transiting through your sun or moon can mean it's a good time to beautify your life somehow. Since the sun is expressive and outgoing, this can mean buying some new clothes or improving your style. On the other hand, the introspective moon can take after Venus' transit and motivate you to beautify your inner worlds, such as by improving your interior décor or furniture.

Mars

The strength, initiative, and courage of Mars' energy usually act as fuel to whatever natal planet, house, or sign Mars is transiting through. In effect, Mars will swoop in and energize the traits of these astrological factors. The transit of Mars is also a time when most people will feel stronger and more energetic, in general. Nonetheless, the very nature of Mars necessitates caution during the planet's transit because tempers can flare up in some cases. This risk is especially high when Mars transits through the natal moon, making for some moody days.

Planetary Returns

Planetary returns are an important factor to consider when reading planetary transits. In the simplest terms, a planetary return happens when a planet traversing across the zodiac returns to the exact point where it had found itself at the moment a person was born. This return marks the end of a major cycle and is strongly associated with new beginnings and grand undertakings in life.

Among the planets, Jupiter and Saturn are the two planets whose returns are considered to be the most important, with Uranus coming in as a close third in terms of importance. It's also important to note that the return of Uranus takes 84 years. Hence, astrologers also give importance to this planet's half-return since many people don't live to 84 years and are thus unlikely to experience the full return.

Jupiter takes around twelve years to fully return, marking an important astrological milestone. Jupiter's return heralds the beginning of something new, such as the next phase in some longstanding, ongoing process. It signals the beginning of renewed growth and development in the broadest sense. Suppose we split a human life according to this cycle. In that case, we can see that it corresponds to some important milestones, such as the beginning of early adolescence at around 12 and true adulthood at around 24 years of age. Jupiter is the planet of good luck. Among other things, the year of its return tends to be a year of overall good fortune. As the planet returns, this is a good time to take the initiative and move toward your goals, as the likelihood of a reward will be high.

Saturn takes around 30 years to make a comeback. Saturn's return is associated with aging and accepting responsibility and change. The cycle of Saturn's return corresponds roughly to the stage in life when many people take on serious responsibilities and make life-long commitments. However, Saturn's return is also associated with new realities and our ability to come to terms with them. This influence may lead some folks to reconsider their earlier commitments. In general, it's when one might decide to take a new direction in life.

Uranus's 84 years to return are long, but this isn't a problem for you because the half-point of that process is considered very influential. Forty-two years into a new cycle, Uranus exerts an influence that can sometimes manifest as self-doubt and major second thoughts, which is why it's associated with the phenomenon known as the mid-life crisis. This can strain long-term relationships, so it's important to cherish your bonds during this time. Despite the stress that the half-return of Uranus brings, this is still strong energy that can refresh and revitalize you and spring you to action. This is why many middle-aged people pick up new hobbies and develop new interests. For those who live to 84 in good health, the full return of Uranus often manifests as a renewed passion for life.

Remember that this was only a quick overview of what planetary transits are and how they might affect you. Transits and returns are major themes in practical astrology, and there is much more to unpack if you want to become an expert on the subject. Still, with this basic overview, you should be able to understand the fundamentals of any upcoming transits that may affect you.

Chapter 10: Planetary Progressions

Astrological or planetary progressions constitute yet another means of predicting events and astrological processes that may occur in the future. Like transits, this is one of the most important tools astrology has at its disposal for horoscopic forecasts. In the simplest terms, an astrological progression is a movement or "progression" of your horoscope from your birth onward based on your birth chart. In a way, astrological progressions describe astrological changes that may occur in your life as you grow older, accounting for your changes in perspective, values, behavior, and so on.

In essence, astrological progression points to the course that a person's life will take. The progressions are read based on your birth chart by looking at what astrologers generally refer to as the progressed birth chart. A progressed birth chart is based on all the same information that a typical chart uses, plus the current date. As such, the progressed chart will show how and where the planets from your birth chart have moved since those placements at your birth. Considering that every sign takes up 30 degrees on the zodiac wheel, we can use the speed at which a planet moves through the zodiac to determine whether it has moved out of its natal sign and how far it has come by your current age.

As with regular natal charts, progressed charts can easily be calculated with online tools. The progressed chart is best viewed as a sort of secondary or auxiliary birth chart that sheds some additional details on your personality and life, particularly concerning how you might have changed during your time on this planet. Astrologers can also make certain forecasts about the rest of your journey based on that. Looking at a progressed chart can lead to surprising discoveries and some interesting "eureka" moments. It's common for people to look up their progressed chart, only to find that it perfectly describes how they changed over the years. These changes often aren't big or dramatic, but they reflect how your life has progressed, especially when it comes to internal things.

Astrological progressions are generally divided into secondary progressions and solar arc direction. This chapter will explain these two kinds of progression and their basics. In both cases, the astrologer looking at a progression chart will read into the changes regarding the astrological houses and zodiac signs compared to the natal chart and the aspects that the planets in the progressed chart have formed with the planets in the natal chart.

Secondary Progression

Secondary astrological progressions are also referred to as "a-day-for-a-year" progressions. Some astrologers also call them major progressions or secondary directions. As their alternative name suggests, secondary progressions revolve around moving your natal chart forward by one day for each year of your life. This is an adjustment of the birth chart by one day for each of the years you're interested in analyzing. For instance, if you're 40 years old and want to see the secondary progression from your birth chart in those 40 years, you'll add 40 days to your birthday and then do a natal chart for that adjusted date. By using the same formula, you can look at the progression for any other point in your life to see how the circumstances of your chart may have changed when you were 20 or 30, for instance.

Following the same logic, you can take a peek into your future self and how the planetary placements will treat you at any point that's yet to come, assuming you live to see that day. It's all about the symbolism of those first consecutive days following your birth as the most formative and decisive time when the universe is hard at work shaping your emerging self. Throughout the field of astrology, most astrologers agree that secondary progressions are the most important type of progression to be analyzed in astrology.

When astrologers look at progressions to make predictions about the future, they use a combination of progressions and transits of the progressed planets to get the most accurate readings regarding specific, important events. In terms of influence, the fundamental difference between transits and progressions is that transits are new, outside-energy influences that the universe throws at you. In contrast, progressions are something already innate and fundamental to your horoscope and charts. Progressions are associated with changes that occur within us; only after that happens do these changes manifest in the outside world. Progressions illustrate major, gradual shifts that go on under the surface all your life – changes that inevitably translate as changes in your real world.

Transits are generally seen as the primary method of predictive astrology, with secondary progressions complementing them. Another thing to remember is that the day-for-a-year formula also translated as a difference in the speed of movement between transiting planets and progressed planets. For every day that a planet takes to transit through the signs, the same but progressed planet will take a year.

As you can see, secondary progressions boil down to a comparison between your birth chart and your progressed chart. The reading of this comparison revolves around looking for a few specific things. If you find that a progressed planet has changed its sign or astrological house, this will be an important change to note. There's also the question of retrograde motions, which we'll explore in a bit more detail soon.

Interpretation, Solar Arc Direction, and Aspects

In many ways, the essence of progressions is to better understand a person's development over time, particularly psychological development, as influenced by astrology. An important thing to remember is that your natal chart dictates certain things that won't change through progression. For example, difficult and tense aspects between two planets in your natal chart can still exert influence even if the progressed version of one of the planets forms a new, positive aspect with the natal version of the other planet. The situation is similar regarding progressed planets that form new aspects where there used to be none in the natal chart.

What all this means is that the pattern of your original natal chart is something that stays with you. It's the foundation of your personality and your relationship with the astrological forces in this universe, and all those eventual influences that come later in life – including progressions – will have to adapt in some way. The transits and progressions that you are exposed to will serve some sort of facilitating role, such as by helping you unlock some of the potential found in your birth chart's pattern or your "horoscopic DNA," as it's sometimes called.

It should also be said that most astrologers give importance to progressions only regarding the inner planets. As you've learned earlier, outer planets already move very slowly, so their movement in a progressed chart will be next to insignificant. However, astrologers will often consider the aspects formed with those outer planets. When progressed, the inner planets have a few characteristics that make their progressions unique. The aspects that these progressed planets form with the planets of your natal chart are one of the main points of interest for astrologers.

The progressed sun, for instance, can be very important to analyze. If you find that the sun has changed its zodiac sign, this progression can tell you a lot about how you've aged. Of course, the traits and characteristics of the signs in question are what you need to consider. Suppose your natal sun was in one of the more introverted signs like Scorpio but shifted into the more outgoing Sagittarius in your progress chart. In that case, this progression can give you some answers about how you've developed from being shy to being more outspoken. The same principle applies to any potential change in your sun's house. Remember that the new positions and aspects are just a subtle evolution and that your natal sun hasn't changed. The core essence of what you are as a person is still there, but your progressed chart will show you how you've evolved and grown from that foundation.

On the other hand, the moon's progression facilitates an evolution regarding emotions, behavior, and a few other things that mostly have to do with maturing. Your progressed moon will be especially important when it forms a conjunction with either your natal or progressed sun, which is referred to as the progressed new moon. This occurrence usually heralds the beginning of a new emotional cycle in your life. Regarding secondary progressions, the moon is one of the most important planets because of its quick movement.

Mercury heralds much-needed changes and adaptations in your life among the three remaining inner planets. It predicts periods of growing intellectual prowess and thinking and a propensity for literature. Travel is also associated with Mercury's progression. On the other hand, Venus pertains to its usual domains involving emotions, creativity, and beauty. When progressed, Venus is associated with important emotional milestones like marriage and new romantic beginnings. On the flip side, it can also spell the end of an ongoing relationship. Major creative endeavors, monetary gains, and childbirth are also possible. Progressed Mars also exerts an influence that's in keeping with the planet's usual themes, starting a period where you'll be energized for increased activity, initiative, entrepreneurship, or conflict. It's a time when restraint and impulse control will be very important since you'll be more prone to accidents, fights, and loss of control.

Besides the planets, some astrologers will also look at the progression of something called angles, particularly the ascendant sign (eastern angle) and midheaven (north angle). These are only used when you're operating on the most accurate information concerning your birth, especially the exact time. Aspects formed by the ascendant and midheaven will affect ambitions, health, self-interest, or anything relating to professional life and careers.

As mentioned earlier, many astrologers use another type of progression: the solar arc direction or progression. This kind of progression is also known as the "degree-for-a-year" progression. Under this method, astrologers will move an entire birth chart forward by a single degree for each year. The formula works similarly to secondary progressions, only with degrees on the chart wheel. It's all about moving the birth chart's planets forward to adjust for the age you're interested in. The method is called solar arc direction because the sun's speed is around one degree daily. Other planets move at different speeds, but they are all made to move in the same fashion as the sun when creating a solar arc progression chart. Solar arc direction isn't used as frequently as secondary progressions, and when it's used, it usually serves as a complementary and secondary chart.

Some astrologers use other progression methods, such as minor, tertiary, converse, symbolic, and ascendant progressions. The main difference between all these methods is the formula by which the progressed chart is calculated and created, but the eventual interpretations of said progressions will follow the same principles as the methods we've just covered.

The Concept of Retrograde Motion

Apart from progressions, another related concept that's very useful in practical astrology is the so-called retrograde motion of planets. A planet's retrograde happens when there is the appearance of a backward motion by the planet, as observed from our own point of view. This happens when Earth moves past an outer planet that's moving slower or when one of the inner planets moves faster than Earth and passes by us. Retrograde motion is a fairly common occurrence for outer planets, as they find themselves in this state more than 40% of the time.

Retrograde motions are generally seen as unfavorable in astrology because they are a movement in the opposite direction of what astrology considers natural. This produces various effects on how these planets act and what kind of energy they'll radiate, often modifying their inherent traits and influences. At the very least, planets in retrograde tend to grow weaker, especially regarding their favorable influences that are diminished. The retrograde motion is analyzed differently concerning secondary progressions and solar arc direction. According to secondary progressions, a planet progression forward by one day actually moves backward on the chart and heads in the counter-clockwise direction.

Stress, difficulty, and tensions are some of the results that most astrologers nowadays associate with retrograde movements. As always, the way these effects will manifest depends on the planets that are in retrograde, taking into account their respective traits. If it's Mars, for instance, issues with aggression or lethargy may occur in some people, just as retrograde Mercury could lead to miscommunication and an inability to express yourself.

However, there are astrologers out there who might interpret some retrogrades differently. Namely, some believe that a planet changing its direct motion into retrograde doesn't have a default effect one way or the other. Instead, these astrologers think that the planet's shift in direction simply affects how a person deals with the area of their life affected by the planet in question. This can go both ways, of course, and the result will depend on many factors that are specific to you. As such, these astrologers view retrogrades and their results as something highly dynamic and changeable. On that positive side of the equation, some astrologers argue that retrogrades can lead to sudden releases of planetary energy instead of repression.

On the other hand, a minority of astrologers don't ascribe that much importance to retrogrades, especially those of outer planets. This is mainly because these planets spend 40% of their time in retrograde. Nonetheless, this is a minority view, and retrogrades are generally an astrological factor that most astrologers take note of when reading charts and horoscopes. As such, it's a good idea to read up more on retrogrades because they are a somewhat complex subject with many different angles to consider. Even among astrologers, some unanswered questions and disagreements about retrogrades still remain. Still, a general consensus stipulates that retrogrades are at least a time to be cautious and warier of your planetary influences acting up. At the very least, this is the way to stay on the safe side.

Step-By-Step Guide to Reading a Progressed Chart

A progressed chart is an astrological tool that can be used to gain insights into your current situation and potential future path. While a birth chart represents where the planets were at the time of your birth, a progressed chart symbolizes the current planetary positions based on your birthday. There are a number of ways to calculate a progressed chart, but the most commonly used method is to progress each planet by one degree for each year after birth. Here is a step-by-step guide to reading a progressed chart:

1. Determine The Planetary Positions

The first step is to identify the planet that is currently in the most important position in your chart. This planet is referred to as the "lord of the chart." The lord of the chart will be located in one of the twelve houses of your natal chart. Each house represents a different area of life, so the lord of the chart can provide clues about what areas of your life are most affected by current planetary influences.

Once you have determined the lord of the chart, you can then begin to look at the other planets in your progressed chart. Each planet will be located in a different house, and each house will represent a different area of life. By interpreting the position of each planet, you can gain insights into the potential developments in each area of your life.

2. Consider the Aspects

Just like in a natal chart, the aspects in a progressed chart can tell you a lot about the energy and dynamics at play in a person's life. The progressed chart is a snapshot of where someone is at a specific point in their life, so the aspects will change over time. For example, if someone has a lot of hard aspects in their natal chart, they may experience some challenges early on in life, but as they get older and these aspects start to soften, they may find that things become easier.

The same is true for someone with easy aspects in their natal chart. They may have an easier time early on in life, but as the aspects start to harden, they may find that things become more difficult. There are many different ways to interpret the aspects in a progressed chart, so it's important to do some research and find an approach that feels right for you. With time and practice, you'll be able to read progressions like a pro!

Different planets will react differently to a change in direction, depending on their circumstances and inherent traits. A particularly influential albeit somewhat rare occurrence is when a planet in transit changes direction shortly after or just as it passes over an important spot on your birth chart. For instance, a transiting planet may pass over one of your natal planets or houses in regular, direct motion, only to enter a retrograde and return across the same point right away. Sometimes, a planet can change direction yet again, crossing the natal point for the third time. This volatile influence can bring about a period of constant change and evolution in your life, for better or worse.

Bonus: Astrological Practice Makes Perfect!

Grasping the theory is one thing, and only half the way, as the next order of business is to apply what you've learned in practice. This holds true in astrology, just as in anything else in life. Practicing astrology is important because it'll really hammer in some of the finer points and help you get a feel for the most important areas of your focus. In time, you'll get a knack for it and become a true amateur astrologer.

Reading your birth or natal chart is a major part of practicing astrology in your daily life, but there are other practical steps you can take as we. Now that we've covered all the fundamentals, we'll wrap things up with some practical tips and ideas for how to start practicing what you've learned this very day.

Exercises in Practical Astrology

Astrology is all about self-care, getting to know yourself, and just overall making your life better. These things should always be the focus when practicing astrology daily. However, the first practical step is to just get better at it. Study and repeat the things you've learned in this book and use them as a basis for further learning. Most importantly, you should practice as soon as possible, as this is always the best way to cement your theoretical knowledge. If you want to learn more, practice, and learn new tricks, one of the best things to do is to take astrology classes or courses, whether online or in real life.

Reading your natal and progressed charts is one of the most common exercises you can take up in astrology. There's only so much to read in your fixed birth chart, though, so it's progressed charts and the tracking of planetary transits that will allow you to spend much more time with astrology. Get thoroughly acquainted with the ins and outs of each planet in even more depth than we've explored in this book, as this will allow you to make it a daily hobby. There's always stuff to analyze regarding the planets, how they move, and where they're going, with all the implications these things have for you. And beyond that, you can and should do the same with other people.

Another great, long-term exercise you can regularly return to is keeping an astrological journal. A journal can be especially useful if you're trying to keep track of your planet's daily transits. This can be a fun hobby that will help you get better at practical astrology, but it will also be a good opportunity to keep a record of how you're feeling and what you're thinking, which can be analyzed from an astrological perspective later on.

Practical astrology can also be combined with other practices such as tarot. Tarot is a whole other discipline you may not be familiar with, but suffice it to say that there are overlaps with astrology. Drawing a daily tarot card is an opportunity to get astrology involved since your card will have a certain astrological correlation. If you practice tarot, then it's a good idea to look these correlations up and see how these two hobbies might complement each other in your case.

General self-care is another place where there is room for astrology. If you have an intricate set of daily or weekly self-care rituals, it might interest you to know that the characteristics and energies of your zodiac sign may make some self-care rituals more important than others. This is worth researching because it can really help you get the most out of your time for relaxation and self-care. That's because different signs benefit from different rituals and have different preferences. Take the contrast between Taurus and Aries as an example. Taurus is typically a sign of serenity and calm, which is why Bulls benefit from quiet downtime involving tea-drinking, scented candles, and similar evening joys. On the other hand, Aries is a sign that's always on the prowl for new thrills, so their idea of self-care is usually very different.

Another exercise that can help you learn more things while also having fun is taking astrological quizzes. The Internet is full of free quizzes that take the input from your answers to a series of questions, apply some astrological principles, and produce results on various topics. Some will take guesses at your near future, while others will try to give you guidance regarding relationships, work, and other areas that may interest you. There are also astrological quizzes that are just there for fun. In general, quizzes won't give you the most accurate readings since they're usually pretty generalized, but they can be a fun little way to engage in astrology.

To a great extent, astrology will be what you make it. All the things you've learned in this book can be applied in various walks of life and to the extent you choose. You have complete discretion over how much you want to commit and how deeply you want to delve into it. As you can see, practical astrology mostly boils down to reading and analyzing things or making adjustments to your life and routine based on astrology.

Extra Tips and Tricks

One of the most fundamental tips you can get in contemporary practical astrology is that you should use online resources. There are many free astrological resources online that can help you not just make a natal chart but also read it. This book has given you the fundamentals to make a basic chart reading, but there's always room for digging deeper.

Various websites have different tools that you can use to get the most personalized and tailored horoscopes that will help you gain deeper insight into your personality and virtually all areas of your life. Some folks use astrology because they're interested in specific areas of their lives, such as relationships, health, or business. Many online resources focus exclusively on these things and allow you to get much more detail than you would through a more generalized horoscope or other astrological reading.

If you're just getting started with astrology, something else you can look for is an astrological dictionary, a few of which are available online. Apart from interpretations and the theoretical subject matter you get from resources like this book, it's good to get an early jump on all of the terminology and lingo astrology is absolutely full of. Once you get a handle on all the terms, it'll be much easier to delve deeper into the more complex concepts and learn more.

It's also always a good idea to get involved with other people with similar interests, especially if you like socializing. Countless people are interested in astrology online and in real life, and they love sharing their knowledge, interpretations, experiences, and ideas. Both novices and experienced astrologers can benefit from this, and it's something you can easily do – thanks to online forums and similar places of digital gathering.

You should look into getting an ephemeris, which can either be bought or acquired on the Internet. This is basically a list or book of all relevant planetary motions that go on every day, which is a great way to determine which planetary transits will be happening and when. An ephemeris can also help you predict planetary returns to plan ahead for these important astrological events. A yearly ephemeris should provide this information for all 365 days, which is plenty to allow you to plan ahead and prepare for important transits.

If you buy an ephemeris such as the printed American Ephemeris, you'll get a lot more in terms of design, additional information, and overall usefulness. However, any free online ephemeris for basic transit analysis will do just fine even for a seasoned astrologer, let alone a novice. Remember that reading the ephemeris in a meaningful way will depend on your understanding of the planets, how fast they move, which signs they are going through, the characteristics of those signs, et cetera. It's certainly a complicated business, so you can see why astrology takes a lot of practice to master.

Without an ephemeris, you can take a look at planetary transits by getting a natal chart done for a future date. It's a sort of cheat you can use to take a peek into the future because you'll be able to compare planetary positions and determine how and where they are moving at the current moment.

Last but not least, remember to use astrology to its full potential. To get the most out of it, apply it to your friends, family, and other people you care about, not just yourself. If there's someone in your life with whom you're trying to connect better or improve your relationship, it's always good to get their birth chart and read through it. Many people are not good at expressing themselves, and even though you've known them for years, many things can go unsaid and unnoticed. Their birth chart will give you a peek into their unexpressed soul, and you'll likely come out with a much better understanding of your loved ones.

Conclusion

As long as you remember that astrology isn't an exact science and won't cure illnesses or solve all your problems while you sit back and relax, it can be a very good friend. It's not just about the advice and guidance that astrology can provide. Engaging in practical astrology will often put you on a path toward realizing new things about yourself and others, which is frequently the perfect push to help you get the answers you need. These answers can help you mend or deepen relationships, make certain decisions, learn important things about yourself, and much more.

As you've seen in this book, astrology has many layers, and it's really up to you to decide how deeply you want to delve into the practice. This depends on what you want to achieve with practical astrology, but in general, even a very casual approach can help you learn quite a few interesting things along the way. The important point to take home is that astrology should be looked to for guidance and insights above all else. If – in the course of your astrological readings – you learn some things about yourself and your outlook that you don't like, you must remember that the course of your life will ultimately be up to you.

One of astrology's stronger points is helping you realize what changes you should make in your life. Self-improvement is a major theme for many folks who get into astrology, and that's undoubtedly a role that practical astrology plays very well. It won't change your life on its own, but it can definitely get the snowball of positive changes rolling, and hopefully, this book will have been a valuable resource by the time you get there.

Part 2: Planetary Magick

The Ultimate Guide to Magickal Spells, Rituals, and Magic Associated with Planets

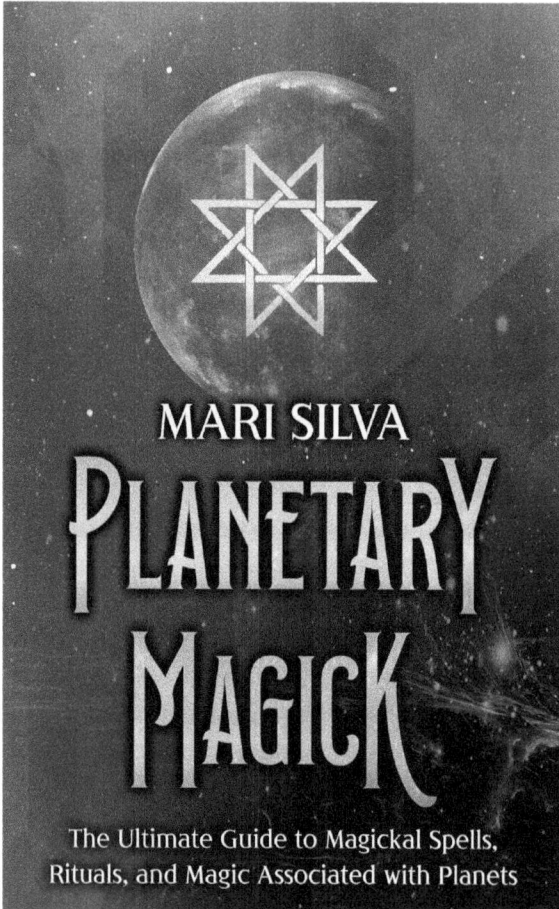

Introduction

What do the planets mean to you? Are they a part of your regular life, or do you just take them for granted? Those spinning balls of energy and mass are part of your universe and influence your life even if you don't realize it. That's like ignoring air and water and the part they play in your daily routine. Imagine a world without the Sun and Moon. Unthinkable right? The other planets in the solar system are just as relevant and influence your daily life.

Learning how and why will help you to tune into their celestial energies to concentrate your focus on their individual strengths and powers. Knowing where the planets were aligned when you were born will give you a unique insight into your personality. The planets know your deepest secrets and will help you become a spiritually and physically rounded human being. Rituals and spells directed to planets and their energies will make you feel connected and part of the astral family. Tap into their energies and get to know them and how they tick.

Horoscopes and astrology have been around since early man looked to the skies for inspiration. Humans have always been fascinated by the heavens, and nothing has changed. Become more involved with astral magick and make your life align with these magnificent energies.

Chapter 1: Planetary Magick Basics

First, don't think that "magick" is a typo. *Magic* and *magick* are different terms, each used to differentiate certain practices within the broader spectrum of magical works. Magic has been used for centuries to describe anything that occurs because of manipulating the physical world with metaphysical actions to create a result.

The term *magick* was first used by Aleister Crowley, a modern occultist who became the face of the resurgence of ancient beliefs, along with Gardner and Hubbard, the founders of modern Wicca and Scientology. He claimed the term "magick" was used to give his beliefs gravitas and differentiate between more serious practices and stage magic. Historical reports of ancient magical powers used the term "magic"; nobody felt they were referring to sawing a lady in half or pulling a rabbit out of a top hat!

Crowley offered several explanations for why he used the alternative term, magick. These included a broader definition, meaning it should be used for any action that helps fulfill any dream, manifestation, or wish that brings the user closer to their true will. He also explained that making the word a six-letter term invoked the magical properties of the hexagram, which played a major part in his writings and spells. Adding the letter K to the word also added the element of the number eleven as it is the eleventh letter of the alphabet. Crowley believed 11 was one of the more significant numbers in magickal workings.

If you study older texts and documents, you will encounter various spellings of "magic," including "majick," "majik," and "magik." Still, they were more influenced by the parlance of the times rather than creating an alternative term. Crowley was the first person to make the term official.

Grimoire Magic

Planetary magic can be traced back for generations and mentioned in some of the more historically significant texts found in grimoires. A grimoire is a term used to describe an ancient book of spells and magic. The name originates from the French term "grammar book," and they were used to record magical spells, incantations, invocations, and other magical works. Some of the more occult-based books focused on the workings of Satan and his demons and encouraged the reader to connect to the darker forces and form an alliance to help them succeed in their lives.

Most grimoires featured the connection between the planets and human life. They recorded how the position of the planets aligned with our lives and influenced how we lived and flourished. Some of the more informative grimoires are still used today to provide information and practices that are still effective in modern life.

Famous Grimoires

The Picatrix

This grimoire was thought to have been written in the 11th century and was named after its author, the wise philosopher Picatrix. It was originally written in Arabic but was translated into Spanish by the King of Castile in the mid-13th century. A Latin version followed, and these were the most studied versions until the early 20th century when the Arabic version was rediscovered by a celebrated German genealogist named Wilhelm Pritz.

The Picatrix is a detailed instruction manual for constructing talismans, combining ingredients to form magical compounds. More importantly – for this book – it was lessons about the planetary spirits and using astrological positioning to dictate when the conditions on Earth and in humankind were suitable.

The volume is split into four books that cover the following areas of magic:

- Book one deals with the heavens and their effects on the beings residing under them.
- Book two deals with the sacred figures in the heavens, the motions of the planets and heavenly spheres, and the effect they

have on earthbound beings.

- Book three deals with the properties and the signs they show us, the colors and forms they contain, and how they affect the Earth.

- Book four deals with the spirits related to the heavens and how they can be incorporated into art or summoned by magical properties using images, smoke, and other methods.

The Key of Solomon

This is a later grimoire thought to have been written in the 13th or 14th century. Although the title would suggest a connection to the biblical figure, King Solomon, or the son of David, it is more likely to have been written by a collaboration of authors who were well instructed in magic and spells. It has several incantations that use the name Jesus Christ which would have been unknown to the biblical figures and, as such, dispels any connection to King Solomon.

It is considered one of the most compelling and inclusive grimoires available and contains two books filled with magical operations. It is a typical example of Renaissance magic beliefs and included nigromancy and geomancy. It gives examples of using air, fire, and water to summon spirits and demons to do their bidding. The books also deal with magical clothing and the implements used to summon the heavens and the otherworld to earthly planes. The Key of Solomon can be found in various languages, and the translations often contain differences in understanding.

The Sworn Book of Honorius

Written in the 14th century, this grimoire was one of the most secretive forms of ancient texts. Each person chosen to receive a copy was sworn to secrecy and swore a pledge to take their copy to the grave. The author is believed to have been Honorius, son of Euclid, and it is believed to have been inspired by angels.

The famous English magician John Dee owned a copy that can currently be found in the British Museum. The book contains some of the oldest spells and incantations to influence angelic and demonic beings to work with humans.

How to Get the Most from Grimoires

Rather than read all the individual grimoires and gain the esoteric knowledge of European scholars, try reading the book "Secrets of the

Magickal Grimoires" by Aaron Leitch, where he provides a comprehensive reference manual of medieval terms. He describes all the different methods and comparisons from around the European continent and the shamanic methods used to connect to the spirits.

The planets and the solar system have influenced society ever since time began. Before the classical planets were named, ancient cultures used the sun, the moon, and the visible planets to worship and praise. The first five planets in the Solar System are hard to date, which means they were discovered and named before official records began.

As Mentioned Above, and So Below

Mottos and phrases are part of modern language and are used to sum up a concept in just a few words. Some of these mottos and phrases are used daily and have an international level of understanding. They mean the same thing wherever you hear them and are part of our everyday speech. They originate from real-life figures or can be part of fictional folklore. For instance, Bob Bitchin is a name that probably means very little to you, but he was quoted as saying, "Attitude is the difference between an ordeal and an adventure." He was wrongly imprisoned and came out of his "ordeal" a changed man. *"People who live in glass houses shouldn't throw stones"* is another saying that is instantly recognizable but came from an epic poem, "Troilus and Cressida."

"As above so below" is another more esoteric phrase steeped in history. It is used when duality is the key component of a relationship. For instance, when the microcosm, i.e., your existence, is measured against the macrocosm, the society in which you live is used to highlight the co-dependence and connections we all need to survive. Another phrase for that situation is "No man is an island."

When applied to planetary magick, the expression goes back to its roots; Hermetic texts were found carved on the Emerald tablet. The Hermetic religion was centered on a prophet called Hermes, a learned sage who prophesized the rise of Christianity. The texts attached to the religion were thought to be a dual form of worship that incorporated the teachings of Hermes, the god of communication, and Thoth, the Egyptian god of wisdom.

The Emerald tablet was part of these texts and is where we can locate the first recorded existence of the phrase "As above, so below," which is connected to alchemy. It refers to the symbiotic connection between nature and the alchemist's work. Astrologers believe the saying is multi-meaning and take the expression to mean that what happens in the Cosmos reflects what happens to the human race. The macrocosm now becomes the heavens and the planets, and the microcosm is the human body. Some experts take that explanation further and believe the connection is between physical and spiritual existence.

No matter what you interpret from the phrase, it is based on the concept that magic and the astral plane are deeply connected. Whatever you do in the physical world will reflect on your spiritual psyche. Whatever planetary forces you embrace will help you form a connection to enhance your life.

A Ritual to Celebrate the Universe

The individual energies of the planets are impressive when considered individually, but as a cosmic force, they are unbeatable. Sometimes we need to recognize the enormity of what they represent when combined. The universe has been evolving for billions of years and should be heralded as part of cosmic working.

Achieving cosmic unity is an energizing process that will help you feel part of the higher consciousness and at one with the universe. The rituals are more powerful when performed under a new or full moon. For maximum effect, perform them during an eclipse.

What you need

- Two black candles
- Two white candles
- Black tourmaline
- Clear quartz
- Pen and paper
- Incense
- Oil burner and your favorite essential oil

Instructions:

1. Clear your altar of any other decorations and adornments.
2. Cover it with a white cloth and place the two black candles at the northern point of the altar.
3. Put the black tourmaline between the candles. Repeat the process at the south of your altar with the white candles and the clear

quartz.

4. Burn the incense and light the oil burner to ward off negative energies

5. Light the two black candles and write on your paper the following:

> "I cast away all the negative parts of my ego.
>
> I surrender my soul to the powers of the universe.
>
> I cast off all my material needs to the universe.
>
> I trust in the universe to help me solve my worries and concerns.
>
> Let my past, my future, and the present be decided by the universe.
>
> I ask for the power of love and enlightenment to fill my life."

6. Spend ten minutes visualizing the negativity leaving your body.

7. Now imagine your old emotions, fears, and worries floating away from your physical body and mind.

8. Feel the light of the universe flood your mind and body and fill it with energy.

9. Use the incense to clear the area of the negativity with smoke. Place the paper under the black candles.

10. Now light the white candles and write on the paper

> "I celebrate my connection to the universe and the light.
>
> I am aligned with the higher beings and their divine energies.
>
> Let the vibrations of the universe resound in my soul.
>
> I am primed to receive cosmic frequencies and energy.
>
> I am ready to expand and become one with the universe.
>
> I am at one with the planets, the stars, the universe, and the binding light."

11. Place the paper beneath the white candle.

12. Sit in front of the altar and stare at the flames of the candles as you reflect on the power of the colors.

13. The black candle represents you letting go, and the flame is clearing all the negativity and emotions holding you back. As it burns, your psyche becomes ready to welcome new consciousness and the high vibrational light of the universe.

14. Stay seated as long as you like and watch the flames, or close your eyes and imagine what your life will look like after the ritual. Imagine the successes you will achieve and the energy flowing into your Crown chakra while your Earth Star chakra is cleansed.

After some time, you will feel the balance of completion when the energies have aligned, and you are ready to end the ritual.

15. Give thanks to the universe and the energies contained in it.

    "This ritual is now complete; I give thanks for your assistance."

16. Blow out the candles and bury the remains in the garden or beneath your favorite tree.

Use this ritual to reenergize your energies when needed and become aligned with the universe.

How Old Are the Planets?

Mercury

The first written recording of the planet Mercury was found on stone tablets dating back to an Assyrian astronomer living in Babylonian times (around 1,000BC) who called it the "jumping planet." The Romans then named the planet "Mercury" after their god of messages because of the speed it traveled across the sky.

Venus

Also recorded in the Babylonian text, it was officially spotted by famous astrologist Galileo in the 17th century. The planet's path led to the discovery that the planets orbit the Sun rather than the Earth, as was previously believed.

Earth

Of course, this planet is unique because we live here and are fully aware of its existence. The shape of the Earth has been and still is the subject of many heated debates, with the first recorded idea dating back to 6,000BC. Even today, the Flat Earth Society has members who argue that the world is not a sphere and is, in fact, flat.

Mars

Ancient Egyptian astronomers recorded the existence of the red planet in 2,000BC. Still, it came to the public's attention in 300 BC when Aristotle recognized that the moon passes in front of the planet, which means it is further away.

Jupiter

The Babylonians mentioned the wandering planet around 8,000BC, but it reappeared in Chinese traditions in 4,000BC when the sky was split into twelve different zodiac regions.

Saturn

This planet is the last that cannot be dated, and the Assyrians made the first record of its existence. They described it as the "sparkle of the night" in 700BC. Galileo believed it was a three-part planet but failed to recognize the rings of Saturn made of rock and ice. This happened nearly forty years after the first official monitoring of the planet.

Uranus

William Herschel was the most influential astronomer of the 18th century and discovered the planet Uranus in 1781. It is commonly called the *Blue Giant* because methane tinges its atmosphere blue.

Neptune

John Adams was just twenty-four when he discovered Neptune, the most distant planet in the Solar System. Unfortunately, he failed to register the discovery, and other astronomers claimed his work. Adams, however, is the official "discoverer of Neptune" and is famed for being the first individual to find a planet using mathematical predictions rather than more traditional methods.

Modern Planetary Magic

When we consider the planets and the solar system, we can easily dismiss them as potential influences and undermine their part in our lives. The planetary concepts we use will often become so commonplace that you forget where they originate. Studying planetary magick helps you recognize how important and influential the planets are and have always been.

We have already discussed their influence on grimoires and the magic practices they contain. Still, there are multiple examples of planetary influence in most religions and traditional magic. Wiccan rituals are often focused on the planets, while Kabbalah and other pagan believers embrace some form of planetary magic and power.

More traditional belief systems focus on the moving celestial objects visible to the naked eye. They employ a classic geocentric cosmos with the Earth as the center of the universe and a series of concentric circles mapped where the planets lay.

Modern planetary magick works with the same philosophy as our ancestors. The celestial bodies in the sky are a miraculous sight even today when more humans than ever before have visited and explored the surface of these planets. Planetary magick is all about exploring the synergy between the planets and humankind and following the patterns they show us.

Planetary magick is concerned with living with these celestial wonders *as if they lived alongside us.* It is all about using rituals, invocations, and talismans to tap into the energy they possess and forming a strong connection through magick to invite them to share their energy to help you achieve your preferred external reality. Don't consider them huge lumps of rock or gaseous solar places in the sky. Instead, consider them as individual states of consciousness or vibrational energy fields just waiting for you to work with them to achieve your ultimate goals.

Planetary magick starts with your basic relationship with the planets and helps you understand how to strengthen ties with your preferred energy sources. The best way to start your journey is by having a detailed birth chart to understand what house you were born in and where the planets were at the time. When you get your birth chart, you also signal your intent to align yourself with the astral plane and begin a new relationship. Like regular relationships, you must let the other party or parties know you are on board.

When you receive your birth chart, it gives you the information you need to decide which planets you feel you are drawn to. You may have a debilitated Saturn in your house, yet you feel like you have a connection with the energies of the ringed planet. You can work on your connection and turn it from a debilitated planet into one of your strongest allies.

The other way to view the chart is to identify which planets are naturally strong in your birth chart and improve the connection you already have. Just like in life, the decision is yours. There is no set map for planetary magick, so be guided by your instincts and prepared for everything you encounter. The energies and powers that come from the planets also have a robust sense of fun and will use that to make your journey to fulfillment a wonderful one, filled with alignments to them.

As you develop your relationships with the planets, you'll become more profoundly connected to yourself. Embrace the gnostic knowledge in your subconscious and become one with the world. You'll become a happier, more balanced, and esoteric being when you let yourself be guided by the astral plane.

Chapter 2: The Planets and You

We have already touched on your relationship with the planets and how important your birth and natal chart help you decide which planets to work with. This chapter is about interpreting your charts and how and when to commission them.

What Are Natal or Birth Charts?

Do you sometimes wish you had an instruction manual for your life? A blueprint to help you navigate your journey on Earth? Here's the good news. You already do! Your birth chart is a picture of the solar system at the exact time of your birth. Think of it as stopping the cosmic clock the second you are born and taking a snap image of the sky at that moment. The image is taken from a prime vantage point: the Earth.

While your birth chart never changes, the influences that affect it do. They are constantly evolving and shifting, and these forces give you indications of which energies to utilize. In the past, birth charts were all hand-drawn and calculated with traditional mathematical formulas. Still, the evolution of online resources means they can be calculated online to allow for daylight saving zones and time variations.

While there are different types of charts, they mostly stick to the same formulaic content. Still, they can look completely different because of their artistic styles. You may prefer a simple design, or you may choose an elaborate style that incorporates all the colors, signs, and zodiac symbols alongside planetary images. The choice is yours, but remember that the information they provide will be instrumental in changing your life, not the stylish look of your chart.

What Does a Natal Chart Look Like?

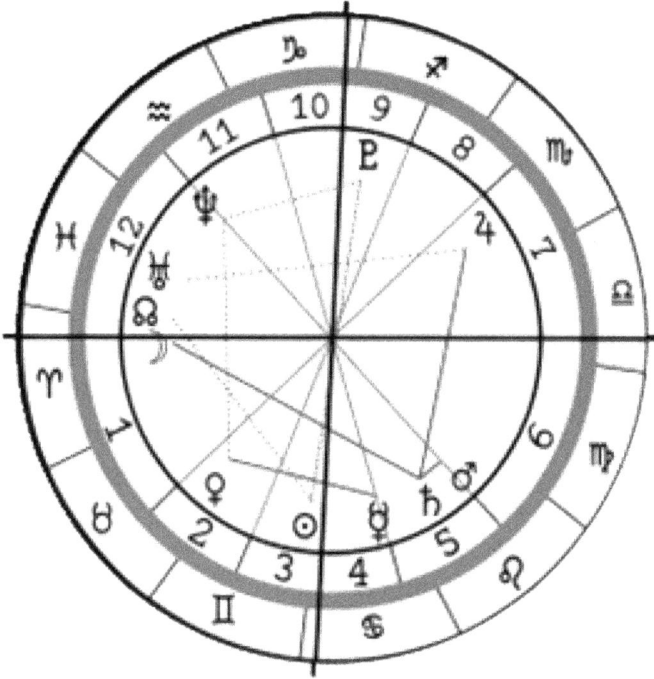

Natal chart example.
Rursus, CC BY-SA 3.0 <https://creativecommons.org/licenses/by-sa/3.0>, via Wikimedia Commons: https://commons.wikimedia.org/wiki/File:Birth_chart.svg

First, you start with a wheel divided into twelve sections to represent the zodiac signs. Each section occupies 30 degrees to complete the 360 degrees of the circle. Now add the symbols in a counterclockwise direction in the following order:

- Aries red for a fire sign
- Taurus green for an earth sign
- Gemini yellow for an air sign
- Cancer blue for a water sign
- Leo red for a fire sign
- Virgo green for an earth sign
- Libra yellow for an air sign

- Scorpio blue for a water sign
- Sagittarius red for a fire sign
- Capricorn green for an earth sign
- Aquarius yellow for an air sign
- Pisces blue for a water sign

The wedges created within the chart are called houses and will be the focal areas of your expression in your chart. An astrologer will chart your birth time and place to create a unique pattern on the chart. If you don't have a definite birth time on your birth certificate, try contacting the Vital Record office in your area or make an estimate close to noon to enter a relevant time. Don't be disillusioned if you don't have a correct birth time; you can still gain information with just your date and location.

Now the astrologer will add all the planet placements at your birth time. They will include the personal planets Sun, Moon, Mercury, Venus, and Mars before the outer planets Jupiter, Saturn, Uranus, Neptune, and Pluto. Depending on the skies, you may include asteroids that were relevant at that time, like Vertex, Juno, or Chiron.

Now you have the basic building block to add to. To create your chart, the astrologer will add a series of lines that link the planets with varying lengths, angles, and colors. They include:

- Elements
- Modes, cardinal, fixed, and mutable
- Signs
- Planets
- Houses
- Aspects
- Nodes, South and North

What an Astrologist Will Look for in Your Natal Chart

- Which house and sign each of the planets is in
- Aspects and angles that are formed between planets

- Identifying any stellium; a point where three planets are in one sign
- The elemental balance
- Qualities and fixed signs
- Patterns formed by the planets
- Areas that need work to create an equilibrium in your life

What Your Birth Chart Will Help You Learn

What Career Path You Should Take

Do you feel like you are in the wrong job and, at some point, you need to seek a new career, but you aren't sure what path that will take? Your birth chart will help you illuminate your future and find a career that suits your strengths and economic requirements. We aren't all fiscally focused, but we all need to earn enough money to live comfortably. Your career path may be so individual that you haven't even considered it in the past. Your birth chart will help you identify your individuality and how you can take this to the workplace. It will also make you more confident to change your life.

It Tells You the Truth about Yourself

It is human nature to focus on people's qualities and gloss over their faults. As a result, we often have an imbalanced view of ourselves and other people. Your birth chart won't sugarcoat your weaknesses and won't inflate your qualities. The detailed information you'll learn will help you work on your weaknesses and strengthen your qualities. Don't take it personally and learn to be more resilient to the truth. The information will help you learn how to recognize who and what to avoid and help you recognize the positive and negative aspects of your personality.

It Will Tell You about Your Three Signs

Your birth chart tells you your Sun, Moon, and Rising signs. You probably know your Sun sign which is your zodiac sign. For example, if you were born on the 6th of April, you are an Aries. However, knowing your Moon and your Rising Sun sign is just as important for your chart.

To discover your true personality, you need to know your Moon sign. This is your instinctual self and is the part of you that tends to be hidden from the world. We all have basic instincts that can be both dark and unexplainable. You can't get rid of them, but knowing what they are will help you grow. Your Moon sign is also the place you retreat to when you need to escape from the stress of everyday life. Some astrologers focus more on the Moon Sign as they believe it gives a truer sense of self.

Your Rising Sign is how people see you at first glance. It is the persona you project to the world and is how you come across. Some people have the same Sun and Rising sign, while others can be polar opposites.

It Will Help You Understand How the Planets Affect Your Energy and Form Your Personality

Your Sun sign is just the first layer of your sense of self. You may have already described yourself as a typical Aries, or when you do something, you say, "That's so like an Aries." However, when you study your birth chart, you discover the very secrets of your soul. That may sound quite dramatic, but it is true. You'll gain a deeper knowledge of who you are and what the alignment of the planets at your birth truly means. On the left side of your natal chart is a list of the positions of all the planets and the dominant zodiac sign when you were born. This gives you an insight into your nodes. The North node will represent the experiences you need to become more spiritually fulfilled. In contrast, the South node shows your natural talents alongside your already mastered skills.

Because the Earth is constantly rotating, the planets are constantly changing houses. Determining where they were positioned when you were born helps you understand why you are drawn to certain people. Others are so foreign to you that they may as well have been born on another planet. Did you know that because of this constant shifting, even fraternal twins born just minutes apart can have completely different personalities?

Your Chart will Show You the Soul Lessons You Will Face in the Future

Your journey through life should be positive and resemble a metamorphosis from a lowly caterpillar to a stunning butterfly, but we all know that doesn't always happen. If you can recognize the lessons you learned in your past lives and employ them in your present life, then you are less likely to fail. You need to identify past traumas and the karma they have attracted so you can move past them. What is in your soul path, and what will you do to make your journey less traumatic and help you reach your goals?

Most people create new charts on New Year's Day or their birthday to help guide them through the next year. These are called transit charts, and a trained astrologer will compare and contrast your original birth chart and the transit chart to help you plan ahead. Having this foresight gives you an insight into what to do and when to do it. If you plan a trip or a special event, you can check with a transit chart to see if the stars are favorable aligned.

Other Types of Charts

Compatibility Charts

Cut through the normal etiquette of getting to know someone by having your charts read. There are two ways to do this; a synastry chart will involve comparing your individual charts for compatibility and contrasts, while a composite chart is a joint effort that compares where you meet regarding your compatibility. The relationship is treated as a separate entity and creates a personality that is a symphony formed by the separate parts of two individuals' psyches.

Annual Forecast Charts

If you have a busy year or want to know when to make significant changes, do a chart that starts on today's date and maps the next twelve months for highlights and pitfalls.

Vedic Chart

If you want an even bigger picture, check out charts that take a different perspective; the Vedic and Chinese astrology charts work with different energies and data, and calculate your chart with an alternative method.

What Are the Planet's Dignities?

Within your chart, you will get a domicile or home position. A planet with Domal Dignity resides in the same sign it rules. When it is placed in the opposite sign to the one it rules, it is described as being in detriment or exile. When it is exalted, it is in a place of awareness, while when it is in fall, it is the opposition of exalted. Don't worry too much about these terms, as we will find out more details when we start to examine the individual signs and planets.

Being aware of the planets' positions will guide what energies you need to use – and which energies need more work. Don't think that finding a planet in detriment or fall is unlucky. It means you'll find challenges, and you may have to overcome obstacles. Is that a bad thing? *The short answer is NO.* By recognizing these adversarial planets, you can approach them with resolve, which builds character and improves your self-esteem.

Working on your detriment and falling planets will take resolve, but it will build your cosmic strength. Think of the work you do as cosmic physical therapy and make your cosmic muscle stronger and more effective.

Exalted and domicile planets are your positive planets; exalted areas are where you can truly shine. The areas that are highlighted are your inbuilt skills and strengths. You may already know your excellent qualities, or they may surprise you. Your chart will highlight what comes naturally to you and where you have a natural well of energy and talent.

Your domicile planets will give you inner peace. They are your kin, and you'll feel completely at ease in the areas they rule. When you and your domicile planets combine, there is a double dose of energy and strength.

The Planet's Effect on Humans

This is just a basic overview of what you can expect in the rest of the book. All the planets play a role in astrology, magick, and predictions. If we break down what our bodies are made of, we find physical elements like atoms that react to chemical and physical effects just like the planets do. There is no doubt that the universe is a thriving mass of connections and elements that cause reactions and effects on our physical beings. Astral cycles and the planets that exist millions of miles above us are all part of a primordial universe where even the smallest atom can be affected by the huge spinning planets in the sky.

Now consider the soul. You may call it your consciousness or your spirit, but nobody can argue that we all have something that makes us spark. Without this metaphysical part, we would just be robots without personalities who merely exist to perform tasks. If our physical bodies are affected by the astral cycles, then doesn't it follow that our souls will react to the gravitational pull, which affects how we think and, in turn, how we act?

The seven planets have physical existence and can be seen. The Sun and the Moon are luminaries that emit light and bring radiance into our lives, while Saturn and Jupiter are slow-moving planets. Each planet has its strengths and powers and is relevant to us depending on its position at our birth and throughout our time on Earth.

We will discuss the more intricate details of each planet later, but here you can get to know the planets as if they were a group of friends, which they will become as you study more planetary magick.

Saturn

This planet is the furthest from the Sun and is known for its cooling and dry energy. It represents older adults and is known as a wise and scholarly planet. In a beneficial position in your chart, it brings wealth and fame, but in a detrimental or fall position, it indicates loss, sadness, destitution, and life hurdles. It is a teaching force that will reward good students and punish those who fail to learn.

Mars

This fiercely masculine planet is defined by its color red. In the descendant, it indicates a technical mind and a short temper. Occupation-wise, Mars indicates careers that need courage and self-confidence, like the military, politics, realtors, construction workers, and surgeons. In the ascendant position, it represents a young mind, but in the descendant, it signifies aggression and anger that can lead to stressful situations and the inability to resolve conflict.

Jupiter

As the biggest planet in the solar system, Jupiter is a kind and benevolent master. If he is placed in a beneficial position, he brings luck and morality and often indicates success and generosity. Priests, teachers, and leaders often have Jupiter as an exalted planetary influence. If he is found in a detrimental position, it can mean depression, pessimism, and fatigue. When a female has Jupiter to her detriment, it can make her arrogant and difficult to live with.

Mercury

This planet governs communication, and when it is in a favorable position, it can mean careers in media, writers, astrologers, and brokers. People with Mercury in the exalted position will be charming and shrewd; they will make good decisions at the right time. Mercury is the planet of logic and will affect reasoning and analytic skills.

Venus

The Morning Star is the planet of love, sex, beauty, and all things creative. It shines brighter than any other planet and indicates careers in hospitality, tourism, the theater, musicians, and artistic and creative trades. The placement of Venus in your chart influences your ability to have a successful love life or relationship, and her energy will help you become more sensual. In a bad position, it means a failure to have successful relationships.

The Sun

As the source of all power, the Sun is the extreme lord and almighty of the solar system. He is the fuel that we all need to live and, as such, in a beneficial position. He brings power and recognition and is often found in a prominent place in the charts of successful politicians and world leaders. In contrast, he brings arrogance and emotional instability in adverse positions that can lead to humiliation and pessimism.

The Moon

The lunar planet is a strong female energy that speaks directly to your emotions and feelings. As the Queen of the solar system, she will bring love, power, financial success, and calm to those in a beneficial position, while she brings depression and pessimism to people who have her in the fall.

The Sun and the Moon are like the eyes of the universe, and they combine with the other five planets to form our universe.

Chapter 3: Shine Bright with the Sun

Where better to start than with the big daddy of the solar system, the boss of the universe, and the power that fuels our life, the Sun, it represents our identity and how we light our own flame in the world, how we shine and how we express ourselves. It represents your relationship with your father and is the star around which all the other planets circle, so the ultimate father figure.

It is represented by a circle of unlimited potential, often with an eye in the center. In some glyphs and symbols, the flames around the sun seem to frame its face and make it seem more human. The dot or eye in the center of the circle represents your focal point and gives you a target to aim for.

While there are no favored zodiac signs, the Sun is a welcome addition to your natal chart, and its Domal Dignity brings great power and prosperity.

The Sun is:

> Domicile in Leo
>
> In detriment in Aquarius
>
> Exalted in Aries
>
> In fall in Libra

Malefic and Benefic Planets

The concept of malefic and benefic planets is an important part of a detailed horoscope, and most people forget to realize there are two kinds of malefic and benefic planets. They can be either functional or natural, and there are certain rules when analyzing their state depending on their relationship with other planets.

The Sun is a functional benefic planet for Aries, Leo, Scorpio, and Sagittarius.

It is a functional malefic planet in Virgo, Capricorn, and Pisces

The Sun is a natural malefic but is not as damaging as the other malefic influences like Jupiter.

These aspects of the planets originally began in Vedic astrology. Still, as we demand more information, Western astrologists have also adopted them to make any readings more in-depth and accurate.

What does the Sun mean in astral terms?

It is your conscious ego and represents your character. If the Sun is strong in your natal chart, it indicates your life path. It rules the heart and the spine and is significant to your inner core strength. When it is strong in air signs like Gemini and Aquarius, it means they believe their thought and beliefs to be as tangible as solid objects.

Key Traits and Personality Types

- **Willpower:** Sun signs will not back down without a fight; they believe in themselves and will fight their corner despite opposition.

- **Determination:** If you want someone to get a job done, ask a sun sign to get on board, any obstacle will be met with fortitude and resolution.

- **Dignity:** Sun signs are proud of themselves and their beliefs but won't resort to bad manners or being rude to get their point across. When confronted with such behavior, they will maintain their calm.

- **Vitality:** Sun signs are filled with energy and ready to get their engines moving whenever you need them.

- **Loyalty:** When you have a friend, they are there for you through thick and thin.

- **Fortitude**: Sun signs can keep going when others have given up, and more importantly, they also inspire others to carry on.

- **Strength:** They are physically and mentally strong and will work hard to keep themselves fit.

- **Positivity:** They have a glass half full type of outlook, and their positivity is catching. You can't be pessimistic in their company.

- **Leadership:** They love to lead from the front and don't have a problem with responsibility.

- **Courage:** They will never back down when faced with problems no matter how difficult the situation and will still go forward even when they are afraid of the outcome.

- **Arrogance**: Because they are super confident and believe in themselves and their beliefs, it can come across as arrogance.

- **Self-Centered:** Sun signs will put themselves first because they believe that is their rightful place. They look after themselves to make sure they are around to help others.

- **Individualism:** They don't play the game like most other people, and they love to buck trends. Sun signs have self-confidence that lets them be individuals, which is the impression they love to give.

While the Sun transits into a new sign every month, it doesn't mean that you change. It does mean that the areas of your life represented by the houses should be acknowledged and worked on. For instance, in the first house, it is in the sign of Aries, which means the focus should be on your physical strength. It tells you to be more active and look after your body by changing your diet and increasing your activities. You are more likely to become interested in changing your look and making yourself look more attractive.

In the second house, it shines on the sign Taurus and is more concentrated on financial matters. It suggests you should rethink investments and purchases that will help you become more prosperous. You may be encouraged to buy key decorative pieces like sculptures and paintings as an investment and personalize your environment.

In the third house and Gemini, it will be focused on your communication skills. You will be encouraged to make yourself heard more and become more vocal in the workplace, improve your communication skills and become more erudite.

Sun Deities

Since the beginning of time, humans have been aware of the power of the Sun and have worshipped deities associated with it. Here are some of the more revered deities from varying cultures:

Celtic Mythology

Grannus, the god of healing springs and spas

Lugh is an Irish deity associated with the sun

Egyptian Mythology

Bast, the cat goddess with solar connections

Horus, the god of the sky and the heavens, whose right eye represented the sun, and his left eye represented the moon.

Ra was the most powerful sun god in Egyptian times

Greek Mythology

Apollo, the god of Olympus responsible for the sun, prophecy, and healing

Helios, the Greek god of the Titans responsible for the sun

Hinduism

Aryaman and Saranyu, the God and Goddess of the heavens, the sun, and the dawn

Surya, the god of solar energy

Mayan Mythology

Ah Kin, the god responsible for driving the darkness out and bringing the sun

Hunahpu was one of the Mayan Hero Twins; he was created as the sun, while his brother was created as the moon.

Native American Mythology

Wi, the god of the sun

Norse Mythology

Freyr, the goddess of the dawn, sexuality, and fertility

Baldr, the god of light

Roman Mythology

Aurora, a powerful goddess of the dawn

Sol, the ultimate sun god

Keywords for Solar Magic

When you are casting spells or creating incantations to summon the sun's power, certain words will help you with your intent.

Use these words to enhance your work and fill it with sun-filled energy

- Bright
- Heat
- Health
- Confidence
- Dawn
- Energy
- Fortune
- Glowing
- Solar
- Deep
- Powerful
- Beacon
- Brilliance
- Coruscation
- Effulgence
- Emanation
- Blaze

Animals Connected to the Sun

The animal world instinctively knows what planet and energy they represent. They are born with an inherent power that helps us connect to them and form unbreakable bonds. Everyone has spirit animals, but most people think they choose what animal to align to. You have no choice in the matter, and your spirit animals or animal totems choose you.

They align themselves to your energy that can be linked to your planetary connections. Knowing you have a strong association with the Sun means you will instinctively be drawn to certain animals. If you are hoping to work with the Sun because it is in a less strong position, you can still use the animal kingdom to learn what strengths and qualities these Sun-connected animals bring.

Some relationships with animals will be seasonal, and that's okay. Just like you change your diet and clothes with the seasons, some animals will be more relevant at certain times of the year. Don't try and force a relationship with them. Just allow them to enter your life when you need them. Solar animals will fill you with inspiration and energy to guide you on your path to self-fulfillment.

Solar Animals

The Ram

Symbol of Aries and one of the most masculine symbols of the zodiac. They represent passion and potency mixed with hot-headedness and a lack of fear. They will rush in without thinking, but they rely on their strength and fortitude. In calmer modes, they are intelligent and creative.

The Salamander

This amphibian has represented fire and light since the times of Greek and Roman mythology. Although it is cold-blooded, it represents fire in myths, and there is an ancient tale of salamanders sleeping in dormant volcanos. When the volcano erupts, it is said to indicate the salamander's wrath.

The Lion

As the king of the jungle, the lion is the obvious animal representation of the most powerful object in the solar system. It is a sign of leadership, courage, and wisdom. When needed, the lion rules with compassion and a strong sense of loyalty and ferocity. He will fight for his territory and pack and protect them with his life.

He also represents the softer side of human emotions and the joy of benevolence. He is the shining gold light in the animal world and is the ultimate protector of secrets.

Rooster

In Eastern cultures, roosters are highly regarded and represent courage and a competitive spirit. They are feisty and courageous, and in Japanese temples, they can often be found running free. The West has embraced the rooster to protect their homes, and they can often be seen decorating weathervanes of door knockers.

Dragons

In Chinese philosophy, the dragon is a master of authority and represents the ultimate connection between animals and mankind. They are warm yet fierce, and they symbolize good luck. Dragons also form a connection with our ancestors, so we can benefit from their wisdom and guidance.

Swans

These magnificent birds may seem unlikely solar animals with their cool white feathers and haughty demeanor. When you observe them in nature, their true power becomes more apparent. They are totally at ease in the water, yet they can soar through the skies confidently. In astral terms, they represent the solar aspect of love and romance. Their grace and beauty will help you when you have troubles in your relationships and need solar guidance.

Spiders

How often has a spider crossed your path, and you have merely brushed it away. Spiders are solar animals and are symbolic of hard work, drive, and achievements. When they appear to you, they are a sign you need help to perform certain tasks you may be struggling with. They help you realize that life isn't always a bed of roses, and you do have to perform duties to help others. Spiders are sent to remind you that we get better results when we all work together.

Peacocks

The noblest example of the avian world, these flamboyant birds are regal and beautiful. They represent the more admired qualities we all want to achieve - glory, vision, wisdom, self-belief, and vibrancy. They shine in a showy yet magnificent way, encouraging us to exude strength and beauty and shine in our own way. They inspire confidence and bring joy and happiness. In North American cultures, peacock feathers are used to treat illnesses and play a role in healing rituals and spells. Medicine men use peacock feathers to awaken spiritual sense and encourage clairvoyance.

Colors Associated with the Sun Signs

As the main source of light, the colors associated with solar power are bright and light. Orange, yellow, and gold are the obvious choices, but you can also use colors associated with dawn and sunset. Pale pink, purple, light blue, and red are also part of the solar spectrum.

Crystals Associated with the Sun

Bloodstone

The bloodstone crystal is the stone of courage and will help you perform protection rituals and spells. It will ground you and give you the strength to speak up when you feel others are subduing you. It helps you work at the moment and banish confusion and negative external forces.

Ruby

This deep red stone brings joy and wealth and unleashes your passion. It is used to bring positivity and laughter. Use the ruby to set your real intentions and achieve your goals. It encourages heart health and confidence.

Citrine

Encouraging creativity and self-confidence stimulates the brain and encourages clear thinking and motivation. Use it to build the confidence to speak out and express yourself without fear.

Clear Quartz

The master healing crystal can harmonize your chakras and help you connect to higher energies. It revitalizes your emotional and spiritual strengths and lets you recharge your batteries.

Metals related to solar energies are copper and gold. Talismans and charms made from these metals and decorated with rubies will bring you strength and good luck.

What Food Appeals to Sun Signs?

Food astrology is a relatively new concept, but if you consider what your natal chart tells you, why shouldn't it include food? You are what you eat, and astrology is just another way to adapt to your planetary self.

If you have strong Sun, you will be drawn to spicy aromatic foods with chilies and ginger. They must be well cooked, and Sun signs don't eat food that isn't both visually and physically appealing. Indian parathas with cumin and mustard seeds will be more appealing than regular bread and served with butter and pickles.

If you want to strengthen your Sun, eat plenty of fruit like oranges, peaches, plums, and pungent foods. Asian food that makes you sweat will help you increase your solar energy. Reduce the salt in your diet to make you feel more energized and powerful.

The Best Times to Work with Solar Energy

Sun magic should be performed when the appropriate time corresponds to the spell.

Sunrise is the time to perform rituals of new beginnings and rebirth. As the sun peeps over the horizon, perform sun rituals to cleanse your spirit and rebirth your energy for the day.

During the morning, you can perform acts that promote harmony and happiness and start to build new plans for your future. Gain positive energy and set resolutions to make your life more prosperous and joy-filled.

At noon, work with the sun to bring magic and health to your household. Noon is also a great time to charge your magical tools and crystals (check they are sun-friendly before leaving them out in the full sun).

The afternoon is time to concentrate on more business-like matters. Work to improve plans for travel and exploring or anything related to your job or career.

Sunset is the time to perform letting go rituals. Relax and let go of stress and depression as the sun disappears behind the horizon and you enter a state of darkness.

How to Cast Solar Magic

Most magical believers are focused on the Moon and the lunar power. Lunar witches love to work in the moon's silvery light, but they are missing out on the powerful strength of sunlight.

Here are some ways to utilize the solar power that appears in your life every day.

Sunbathing

UV rays are healthy, providing you stay sensible. Solar signs feel depressed when they don't get sunlight, so make yourself get out and about in that healing sunshine. Lay on the grass and turn your face to the sun. Wear sunscreen and glasses to protect your skin and eyes and bask away!

Sun Water

Everyone knows the power of moon water, but solar water is also perfect for cleansing your altar, tools, and yourself. Leave a glass container filled with water in the sun to charge, and then add it to your bath water for a refreshing and cleansing soak.

Fill Your Space with Sun Plants

If you have a garden, grow plants connected to the solar and fire elements. Daisies, sunflowers, rosemary, and rue are all simple to grow and thrive in ordinary soil or pots. If you don't have a garden, choose house plants that will connect you to solar energy.

Drink Sun-Based Iced Tea

When you have been sunbathing, you need to replete your system with water. Why not make that drink even more magic by infusing it with sun-based herbs and infusions. Take a glass jar and partly fill it with water. Add stevia, mint, an herbal tea bag, and a sprig of chamomile. Screw the lid tight and leave it in the sun to brew for two hours. When it has cooled, pour it over ice, and drink it. It is both magic and good for you.

Work on Your Solar Plexus

The mass of nerves at the pit of your stomach can be thought of as the control center for the organs in your abdomen. Solar energy is especially important for the solar plexus as it is the third chakra that is governed by the sun. Strengthen it with exercise and regular stretches to make sure it stays healthy and keeps your abdomen functioning.

Create Sun-Based Crafts

Make sun catchers and prisms to hang in your home. Use the colors connected to the sun and catch the light. If you prefer kitchen magic, use plants and foods linked to the sun. Create sun-shaped bread or use sun-dried tomatoes to make your food tastier.

The Sun is with us every day, yet we take it for granted. Use solar connections to make your life more joyful and illuminated.

Chapter 4: Go Over the Moon with Magic

In astrology and magick, the moon is the mother of the universe. She is the power behind our most basic natures and survival instincts that are so embedded we don't acknowledge them. It is the planet of emotions and feelings, and when you work with lunar magick, you'll strengthen both your physical and psychological well-being.

It is the largest satellite in the universe and is intrinsically linked to the Earth. No matter where we are in the world, we always see the moon's same face due to the gravitational pull and the alignment of orbital periods. It is linked with the Sun to create a celestial duo representing the ultimate duality as the day disappears and turns into night. This seemingly effortless transition means the two are symbolic of the upper and lower worlds. The Moon is the feminine half of the union and is linked to all feminine aspects. She is the regulator of women's cycles and the fertility of females and crops.

Signs of the Moon

Lunar phases.
See page for author, CC BY-SA 4.0 <https://creativecommons.org/licenses/by-sa/4.0>, via Wikimedia Commons: https://commons.wikimedia.org/wiki/File:Lunar_phases.svg

The traditional glyph is the crescent moon, but as the moon has many cycles, it also has glyphs to represent the various cycles. The crescent is the waxing moon and represents the second cycle. The eight cycles are as follows:

1. The new moon is represented by a full circle with a four-pointed star in the center.
2. The waxing moon is represented by the crescent moon facing left.
3. The right half of a circle represents the first quarter.
4. The crescent moon represents the waxing gibbous with the curve pointing upward.
5. A full circle represents the full moon.
6. The waning gibbous is the crescent moon pointing downward.
7. The last quarter is the left half of the circle.
8. The waning crescent has the crescent moon facing right.

The Dignities of the Moon

The moon is in domicile in Cancer

In detriment in Capricorn

Exalted in Taurus

In fall in Scorpio

The moon is generally a benefic planet and brings prosperity and life to the Earth. It is by nature beneficial and works with the sun to create both malefic and benefic atmospheres depending on the transit positions of the other planets. It is the fastest moving planet and will only spend two days per month in the zodiac houses, making it even more important to pinpoint these times and use the time well.

The Traits of the Moon

Strong moon connections indicate a caring, complex personality that is emotionally transparent. They may wear their heart on their sleeve, but they are compassionate and invested in the well-being of others.

When found in the water signs, it signals a deep and complex mother figure who naturally cares for others. They exhibit empathy and have vivid imaginations that fuel creativity and artistic skills.

In fire signs, the Moon is a sign of a mother who encourages her offspring to get out in the world and explore. They understand that courage and strength will help others to become worldlier and broaden their horizons.

In earth signs, they are more likely to manifest as a traditional mother figure who believes that routine and security are the bedrock of life. They feel responsible for others and often sacrifice themselves to care for others.

Moon in air signs means a communicative mother who loves to tell stories. They are filled with stories and tales of magical places and wonderful people who inspire free expression.

Moon Deities

Most Western societies associate the Moon with female energies, but that hasn't always been the case. In Egyptian and Eastern cultures, the Moon was represented by male deities. Here are some of the better-known lunar gods and goddesses:

- In Greek mythology, Artemis was the goddess of the moon, but in earlier teachings, the moon was represented by Selene.
- Thracian teachings also had the goddess Bendis who ruled alongside Artemis and was favored by more formal and classical teachings. She was popular in Athens in the 4th century and appeared on pottery and in sanctuaries carrying two spears ready for the hunt.
- In Mexico City, a monument to the moon goddess Coyolxauhqui was discovered and is thought to represent her dismembered body following a battle against her brother and archrival, the sun god Huitzilopochtli. She was the Aztec goddess of the lunar realm.
- Romans worshipped the goddess Diana, the Roman equivalent of Artemis, and was also known as the goddess of the hunt. She is often pictured with a bow and arrow and flanked by a woodland animal like a deer.
- Heng-o is the Chinese moon goddess and resided in a huge white palace built from ice and snow. She is clothed in white and silver robes and wears white jade jewelry. She has a male counterpart named Thearch, who is said to represent the male soul of the

moon.

- Khonsu and Thoth were the Egyptian deities of the moon. The Egyptians believed that a huge white baboon lived on the surface, and the moon was created from the left eye of the god Horus. Isis was the female counterpart to Thoth.

- Tsuki-Yomi is the Japanese moon god and was the sibling of the sun goddess. In mythology, he killed another god because he offended his sister, but she didn't agree with his actions, which explains why the two planets are so distant.

Keywords for Lunar Magic

- Iridescence
- Beams
- Silvery
- Emotional
- Sparkling
- Pine
- Satellite
- Natural
- Cycle
- Infinity
- Pearly

Moon Elements

Colors associated with the moon are blue, white, silver, and soft pink. They are the colors from nature, but you can also use the colors of the Sun because the two planets will always be linked. Yellow and orange will help bring warmth and energy to your magick and a perfect combination of light and darkness.

Moon herbs include frankincense, tea tree oil, mint, citrus, myrtle, and sage.

Crystals for lunar magick should correspond to the different cycles and are especially effective when used correctly. Here is a guide to the cycles and crystals and how they work in unison:

The New Moon

The new moon is the first cycle and offers a blank slate to set your intentions. Use the crystals to perform rituals to cleanse your mind, set new goals, and inspire yourself to succeed.

Black obsidian is filled with reflective energy that highlights your inner thoughts and hopes. Use it as a mirror to see inside yourself and focus on what you need.

Labradorite is the Ying to the black obsidian's yang. It brings an energy of magic with flashes of light and possibility. It creates an end to the darkness and attracts magic and light.

Manifest your intentions by writing your goals and intentions down 108 times on paper while focusing on your crystals. 108 is connected to the energy of the moon and represents completion. Anoint the paper with your favorite oil and place a white candle on top.

The Full Moon

Now is the time for some mental housework. The full moon's bright light will help you decide which of your intentions are still worth pursuing. Use these crystals to illuminate your magick:

Moonstone does what the name suggests and connects you to the powerful guidance of lunar energy and makes your path obvious. You'll be filled with the spiritual energy to help you achieve your goals and manifest your needs.

Selenite helps you tap into higher energies and capture the powerful beam of the new moon.

Clear Quartz gives you a clarity of thought that lets you work with increased energy and focus.

Crystals for the First and Third Quarter

These are periods of transition, and you should be focused on combining the dark and light energies you will encounter.

Tourmaline quartz is the perfect counterbalanced crystal to help you check in on your successes and potential failures. Don't be disheartened by any negative aspects; just decide if you want to work harder on them or assign them to the wastebasket of intentions. There is nothing wrong with recognizing that some goals aren't for you. That's human nature; we can't all be experts in every field.

Moon Oil Recipe

You can use moon oil to increase its potency when you set your intentions on paper. Use this recipe to create a fragrant and powerful oil to anoint your altar and work.

What You Need:

- Gardenia essential oil
- Lotus essential oil
- Jasmine essential oil
- 15 ml carrier oil like almond or avocado

Instructions:

Take three parts gardenia, two parts lotus, and one part jasmine and combine with the carrier oil.

Lunar Animals

The animals associated with the moon are defined by creatures that draw their attributes from lunar energy. Alchemists work with the connection between water and the moon, while astrologists focus more on the zodiac sign, Cancer. The animals below are indicative of a combination of these qualities and strengths. They are quite often nocturnal and rely on the moon to light their regular environment. Lunar animals are linked with fertility, strong maternal bonds, and are receptive to humans.

The Owl

One of the most symbolic animals associated with the moon, the owl represents wisdom and adaptability. They can survive in the most adverse situations, and they are calming and balanced.

The Wolf

Often depicted howling at the moon, these magnificent canines have a keen sense of the dark. They are one of the ultimate predators and hunt both alone and in a pack. In mythology, they are the monsters that men turn into in the moonlight, and werewolves are intrinsically linked to the moon. Whatever environment they find themselves in, they can use nature to thrive. Wolves are found in all types of terrain and seem to be able to make it habitable.

The Bat

These nocturnal creatures are also the symbols of evil with their association with Dracula and vampires. They are creepy-looking and fly instinctively, so they are successful hunters and survivors.

The Crab

This aquatic organism is naturally associated with the moon via the zodiac Cancer. It can exist on land or in the water and is adept at moving and avoiding obstacles. This symbol signifies you need to be more objective and sharper with your thoughts. Widen your horizons and be brave. Sometimes the crab is sent to you to warn you of negative forces. Watch out for people who aren't as genuine as you thought, and be aware you may have to put on a brave face and deal with them.

When you dream about crabs, the color is important. If you dream about a red crab, it means you are keeping your emotions bottled up. Let go of any resentment or anger toward someone who is currently causing you grief. Let them go. If you dream of a white crab, it means you are in a place where you can embrace love and relationships, life is sweet, and you are getting the go-ahead to make major romantic decisions. If you dream about a dead crab, it means you are in crisis. It's time to regroup and get your affairs in order.

The Dolphin

If you have ever swum with dolphins or seen them in the wild, you will understand the sheer joy of these animals. They are majestic and unthreatening, yet their laughter fills you with the wonder of nature. They are playful and generous and have a majestic sense of peace. They are intelligent and social, just like humans, and they bring the value of friendship and community.

Dolphins are mammals that live in the sea, so they represent the duality of land and sea. They have solar and lunar traits and are known as the princes of the sea. Call on dolphins to bring positive energies and grace into your life and make you feel better when you are unhappy. Dolphins work together to achieve their goals, and they are sent to you when you need to seek help from others. They remind you that although you are capable of great things alone, you can also work well as part of a team.

Dolphins mean different things in different cultures and Celtic beliefs: they are the sacred guardians of the seas, while Christians believe they are instrumental in transporting souls to heaven. Greeks and Romans often depicted dolphins as companions to their gods like Neptune, Eros, and

Cupid.

When dolphins dive across your path, they bring you joy, happiness, and the reminder to make your life more balanced. They will visit you when you are too concentrated on serious matters to remind you to spend time with your friends and family. If you dream about a dolphin in clear water, you have a balanced life, while if they are in murky water, you need to address the negative relationships in your life.

Foods That Relate to the Moon

Because the moon is responsible for your root chakra, you will experience back pain and increased lethargy if it is imbalanced. You will feel depressed or anxious and will be easily distracted. Eat foods that boost your chakra, like:

Root Vegetables

Parsnips, carrots, garlic, beets, and potatoes should be a daily staple. Drink dandelion tea or add turmeric to your diet to increase your energy and feel more at ease in your skin.

Hot Peppers

Red cherry peppers, bell peppers, serrano, and chipotles will add fire to your food and increase your physical zing. They will help you become more aware of the physical aspects of your body and encourage you to exercise.

Red Meats

Iron and protein are important to nourish your root chakra, and red meat is a key source. Eaten in moderation, organic beef, lamb, and venison will immediately energize your chakra.

Eggs

Eggs also contain protein and minerals to strengthen your chakra.

High Protein Foods

If you are vegan or a strict vegetarian, you still need to get your protein, and these foods are rich in protein but still vegan. Tofu, beans, peanuts, cashews, seeds, and organic nut butter will help you feed your root chakra.

Red Foods

Your root chakra will benefit from all naturally red foods like apples, rhubarb, tomatoes, cranberries, and grapes.

Moon Rituals for Everyone

When starting your magickal connection with the moon, it is best to work with the full moon. Lunar energy is abundant, which means your rituals are more likely to work.

Full Moon Ritual

1. Sit in the light of the full moon, either inside or outside.
2. Make sure the space is free from clutter and ready to receive natural energy.
3. Light a white candle and close your eyes.
4. Concentrate on your breathing and take a blank piece of paper to record your experience.
5. Write what you feel is holding you back. For instance, *"I need to let go of a past relationship."* List as many items as you like and add as much or as little detail as you choose.
6. Now write a list of things you want to attract. For instance, *"I want to gain a promotion at work."* And do the same with this list.
7. Remember that list is for your eyes only and will never be seen by anyone else. Once it is completed, sign and date it. This is your sacred contract with the universe, and it is fueled by lunar energy.
8. Now read it out loud and say the words with conviction. Repeat any salient parts you feel need extra emphasis and give it your all. Take a deep breath but make sure you complete the task with force and enthusiasm.
9. Now destroy the contract by burning it or ripping it into small pieces. Wash your hands in clear cold water and dry them thoroughly.

Ritual to Embrace the Maiden, the Mother, and the Crone

The moon is often depicted as a three-part deity. It represents the three ages of females and can be seen as negative. It is important to remember that not all maidens are young, not all mothers have children, and not all crones are old. They aren't determined by age and are determined by energy.

Maidens represent purity and the creative force. They are a symbol of new beginnings and growth. Mothers represent the sexual force of birth and the protective energy that shouldn't just be restricted to children. She embodies nurturing qualities and protection and also stands for fulfillment and creating new life.

The crone is the embodiment of transformation and wisdom. Use her energy to end situations and move on to new projects. She is wise and dark, but her age isn't relative. Help yourself deal with grief or any sense of loss and draw on her energy to move on.

Reach out to female friends to join you in this ritual and represent the ages of women if you can ask nine women to dress in white and carry nine white candles to represent the maiden. Now gather nine women dressed in scarlet to represent the mother carrying white candles with red ribbons to represent the mother. Finally, nine women dressed in black carry white candles with black ribbons for the crone.

Ask the women to say something about the age of the women they represent. Honor all stages and remember to mix the ages of the women involved. Light the candles and watch them burn as you all share the joys of womanhood.

If you are performing a solo ritual, create a sacred space and close your eyes. Repeat the phrase *"I am the maiden, the mother, and the crone. Sacred moons fill me with your light and show me my path."* Be receptive to the energy that will come your way and celebrate your feminine being.

Chapter 5: Mercury, Your Mind and Mouth

Mercury is the closest planet to the Sun and is the smallest in the universe. It may be smaller than its counterparts, but it is just as important as some of the bigger planets that influence us. Think of Mercury as the small, scrappy fighter with a lightning-sharp wit and a skilled communicator in your group of friends.

The glyph for Mercury is a circle with a cross on the bottom and an upturned crescent moon on top. It is like the glyph for Venus and strongly indicates feminine strength and traits.

> Mercury is in exaltation in Virgo
>
> In Dignity in Gemini and Virgo
>
> In detriment in Sagittarius
>
> In fall in Pisces

It is considered benefic when alone or with Taurus, Gemini, Aquarius, Virgo, and Capricorn. When associated with the other signs, it can be malefic.

Benefic Effects Include

- Mimicry: They are good copycats and love to entertain people with their impressions.

- They also adapt other people's ideas and make them their own. They realize that their skills lie in recreation rather than coming up with original ideas.

- They know how to work the system and will claim every cent they can from the government and other agencies. After all, they are entitled to it. They will also find ways to cheat banks and avoid paying back loans.

- They make great advisors if you are in business as they know every loophole and tax avoidance scheme known to man. They are skilled at running operations under other people's names and keeping their names clean in case things go wrong.

- They will use the law to punish their enemies rather than confront them one to one. They hate criticism and can be petty about those who dare to disagree with them.

- They are financially focused and would even change their identity and adoption if it meant they would benefit from an inheritance.

Effects of Mercury in the Malefic

- They can't be trusted to find work for themselves. They need someone else to hold their hand and show them where to find work.

- They won't travel alone even though they communicate well in all languages.

- They project an elevated level of knowledge about things they barely know anything about.

- Restaurant food is wasted on them; they prefer fast convenience food and don't understand the joy of eating out.

- They are scruffy and don't have the best hygiene regime.

- They believe they are indispensable in their job and love to tell people how important they are.

- They lie with alacrity, and even when they are caught in a lie, they will still maintain they are telling the truth.

- No matter what the ruling party is, they will disagree with their policies and methods.

- They talk about their ambitions, but they live hand to mouth in reality.
- They expect other people to sympathize and show empathy, but they have no time for other people's problems or troubles.

Astral Traits

Other traits that are shown by people with Mercury in their sign:

It is primordial. Mercury grows and changes when it encounters other elements, and so do people who have it in their astrological makeup. They will absorb qualities and skills from others and adapt them to suit their needs. This isn't a bad trait providing they acknowledge the source of information and don't try and claim it as their own.

They are born communicators and are quick to process mental thoughts and ideas into speech. Their quick-wittedness and intelligence make them good company, but they do tend to be capricious. Multi-tasking comes easily to them, and they can handle multiple issues providing they aren't required to be too detailed. They get bored with subjects and move on without finishing them properly.

Their intuition and logical thinking mean they are suited for careers in transportation, commerce, tourism, logistics, technology, and commerce. Thieves and tricksters will also tend to have a strong connection to Mercury. They have a quick temper but don't hold grudges.

Because it is so close to the Sun, it is a reinforcing element that encourages self-exploration and development. When it is combined with other signs, it produces the following:

With the water, signs strengthen empathy and increase emotional intuition.

Fire signs make cautious people bolder and encourage them to make themselves heard. It gives them a strong sense of self-confidence and helps them become more open with others.

Earth signs teach the person to concentrate more and daydream less. The practical side of their personality is encouraged to emerge.

Air signs encourage a more expressive personality that can speak swiftly yet confidently.

Deities Associated with Mercury

One particularly important deity is a correspondent of Mercury, and that is Hermes, the exalted one and the divine messenger. Hermetic magic is the belief there is monotheism but describes the three realms of understanding and promotes certain thinking methods. The main philosophy included the phrase "as above so below" that we have already covered, but there are some other key points you may find interesting.

Creation is good, and stagnation is evil. This is one of the more contentious parts of Hermetic teachings that suggest that only God is truly good. Humans have physical forms and will forever be focused on material needs rather than spiritual improvements. The source of ideas can be both good and evil, so the source is the key to living a better life.

God is "All": This statement strengthens the belief that no matter how many spirits or angels we believe there are that God has both transcended reality and is reality.

There is a single truth: The same principle fuels all beliefs, no matter your religion. The Hermetic teachings hold there is just one truth that all humanity should follow.

Reincarnation: Hermetic texts contain written evidence that it believed in reincarnation; we all live many lives on earth to reach a closer relationship to the Divine being, God.

In Hindu Religion

Ganesh has multiple epithets, including the Giver of Good Counsel, the Teacher of Prudence, and Friend of All.

In Egyptian beliefs, Mercury is associated with Seshat, the goddess of Heaven and the Mistress of the Sacred Characters. She was responsible for recording the passage of time and establishing celestial alignment.

In Norse Mythology

Mercury is associated with the mighty Odin, the Father of all Gods and Men. He was the shaper of Wyrds and existed on a mental plane that transcended the Earth and was constantly seeking wisdom and knowledge. He sacrificed an eye at the well of Mimir to become more knowledgeable, and his fate was sealed when he hanged himself for becoming the master of the Ancient Runes.

Loki is also linked to Mercury as they are both imbued with trickster qualities. They share an energy that can be amusing yet frustrating and is often distracted from their original goals by others.

Celtic Mythology

Esus, also known as Gaul, was the god of human sacrifices and associated with Mercury and Mars. He was pictured with an ax and is regarded as a woodcutter in mythological terms. His sacred animal is the bull.

Associations of Mercury

Her feminine power is related to the masculine color blue but with softer tones. Pigeon gray with blue flecks, sky blue, light blue, and violet are also favored.

Work with diamonds, jade, jasper, topaz, tourmaline, and opals to strengthen your magick.

Herbs to include in your work include cassia, clary, dill, fennel, hazel, and Irish moss.

Mercury Oil

Take one part parsley, two parts dill, and three parts fennel. Grind the herbs or seed in a pestle and mortar before adding them to a carrier oil like olive or almond oil. Use to anoint your candles and altar or other magick tools.

Keywords Associated with Mercury

- Reasoning
- Communicating
- Exploration
- Intelligence
- Knowledge
- Patriotism
- Cultural
- Independent
- Thoughtful
- Strategic
- Cunning

- Sneaky
- Written word
- Colloquial
- Expressive
- Gossip
- Untrustworthy
- Memory
- Logical

Animals Corresponding to Mercury

The Fox

Cunning and quick, this wiry animal embodies the spirit of Mercury. They live nearby but are often invisible until they wreak havoc on your home. They steal eggs, kill chickens right under your nose, and escape in the wind. Foxes are also sneaky and leave very little trace as to where they live.

The Serpent

Most people dread the serpent, but a serpent represents rebirth as snakes can shed their skin and emerge as new creatures. They also represent balance and diplomacy that helps you to avoid becoming judgmental. It is a vigilant and intuitive animal and dictates that you stay grounded even in chaotic circumstances.

If you dream about a snake biting your arm or leg, it can signal a financial loss. If the snake is chasing you, it means you have someone in your life who is setting off alarm bells. Dreaming about killing a snake means you are getting stronger, and you will soon overcome any problems in your life.

Swimming with snakes in your dreams means you are going along with other people for the moment and that suits you just fine. If a snake is wrapped around your body, it signals you are frustrated by life and need to break free from repression.

The Ant

This diligent creature doesn't get anywhere unless it puts in the effort. It might be diminutive, but it has immense strength and can accomplish great feats. It is a social animal that works best as part of a team but can also be effective as a solo operator. If you dream of ants, it means you are overwhelmed by minor nuisances that are forming to become a huge problem in your life. The ant tells you to tackle the small stuff and eat away at the minor niggles.

The Spider

Another industrious creature, the spider symbolizes patience, creation, inner growth, and creativity. It is the epitome of creating beauty from the most basic materials and making plans for your life. As they have multiple eyes, they symbolize caution and a natural sense of danger. You know the world is dangerous, but you know how to survive.

You have excellent coordination and love to organize your home, life, and other people. You have a gentle touch and are kind even when you are firm with others. In dreams, spiders represent a lack of representation in your social life. Get out there and be yourself rather than hiding in the shadows.

The Monkey

Playful yet intelligent the monkey is a kind and curious creature that thrives in families. It has a strong sense of belonging and has delightful untamed freedom while still observing social edicts. As your spirit animal, it signifies your ability to make jokes and entertain your many friends, but you can sometimes be insensitive and hurt their feelings.

The monkey is a friendly creature that can become defensive and aggressive when threatened. You have a strong sense of community and will protect those you love with your life. If you dream about monkeys, it may be time to get serious and leave your playful nature at home, where you can be as silly as you like.

The Coyote

The trickster of the natural world, a coyote, symbolizes your enthusiasm and fearlessness. Coyotes are filled with a strong intelligence coupled with a childlike manner that will help you find the magic of life through paths that may be hidden at the moment.

You are quick-witted and determined to find the positives in all situations. When you make a mistake, you are quick to own up and laugh at yourself before trying again. Playing practical jokes is one of your specialties, and you can sometimes take them too far. If you dream about a coyote, it can indicate a spiritual shift in someone you know; are they deceiving you? It could be a sign of disloyalty by others.

How to Work with Mercury Energy

The best day to work with Mercury is Wednesday, but don't forget to call on it whenever you feel you are struggling with communications. Divine energies are available whenever you need them.

Cast Communication Spells

1. Take a sheet of yellow paper and some light blue candles.

2. On the paper, write the name of the person you find it hard to connect to.

3. Fold the paper three times as you repeat the phrase, *"Miscommunication should go for good; with this spell, I will be understood."*

4. Now seal the paper with some wax from the candle and keep it like a sealed letter.

5. Bless it with Mercury oil and repeat this phrase *"Ideas and words will flow to me, and help me say my words, truth, and love I give for free; they fly from me like birds."*

6. Carry it with you and use it when you feel you need help being understood.

Cast Call Me Spells

1. Repeat the last spell but write the name of the people or person you want to call you.

2. When you have blessed the paper, bury it under your favorite tree and bless the ground with Mercury oil.

Cast Manipulation Spells

Mercury is powerful energy to manipulate someone to bend their will. Remember, magic should never be used to cause harm or change their consent status, but it can be used to give them a gentle nudge to see things your way.

1. Use blue candles and your favorite Mercury-related stone to set the tone.

2. Compose a chant about what you want and who needs to be manipulated and repeat it until the candle has burned for five minutes.

3. Take the candle and wax, wrap it in a white handkerchief or cloth, and keep it in a sacred place.

4. Once the spell has worked, bury the package in the ground.

Use Meditation to Connect to the Energy of Mercury

The astral energy will help you become more adept at communicating and becoming a more effective personality. Mercury retrograde meditations are specially designed to help you become an accomplished empath. The term retrograde refers to words you should reflect on and provide you with a grade A form of mediation.

Follow these simple steps to connect to Mercury and ask your relevant questions.

Step One: Make yourself comfortable and clear your mind. Take deep breaths until you can hear and feel your heartbeat.

Step Two: Check your reactions: Be prepared to take a giant step back if something controversial happens. This type of meditation can be challenging.

Step Three: Check your throat chakra is relaxed. Mercury relates to your throat chakra, so be prepared for some tension there. Make sure you have a soothing drink to aid your relaxation.

Step Four: Remember who you are and what your life purpose is. This can be challenging as we get so caught up in our daily routines we lose sight of what we really want. Ask yourself what your true purpose is and if you are on the right track.

Step Five: Reflect and rest. Do you make time for yourself, or are you so caught up in life you don't get time for yourself? Add more relaxing activities to your schedule. Add a date night if you have a partner, or just make time for yourself. Breathe deeply and remind yourself why you need to recharge and regroup.

Step Six: Have some fun. Come up with a new life plan which includes fun activities. Get creative and start new projects. Remember what you used to love as a child and try out that activity again. Coloring books and simple games like skipping or hula hoops are the perfect way to revisit your childhood.

Finally, remember to meditate and relax more no matter where you are or how much time you have. You don't need a quiet mind to meditate. You just need a couple of minutes to switch off. Remember that Mercury and her energies will help you discover the joy of self-communication and more traditional ways of interacting.

Chapter 6: Mars, the Victorious Leader

Mars.

The planet Mars represents the very essence of your being. Its glyph is a circle with an arrow pointing to the upper right section of the sky that symbolizes the human will surmount with the arrow of desire. As the red planet, it has called out to humans to visit for years, and when we eventually managed to land a vehicle on the surface, we weren't disappointed. It may only be half the size of the Earth, but it has impressive valleys and peaks that make the surface a wild and wonderful terrain.

In astrology and magick, Mars is filled with passion and dynamic energy. The energy it creates inspires self-confidence and the belief that anything you want can be achieved. It defends itself with vigor and is self-serving energy that helps you get what you want.

> Mars is in exaltation in Capricorn
>
> In dignity in Aries and Scorpio
>
> In detriment in Libra
>
> In fall in Cancer

When it is dominant in water signs, it makes the person prone to weak willpower even when they are in a strong-willed sign like Cancer

In signs of the fire element, it causes periods of anger and passion. It influences people to let their self-assuredness go one further step and become aggressive. It can lead to disruptive relationships which begin with absorbing passion but end with heartache.

When it is in the earth element, there is a more simmering passion boiling beneath the surface but is explosive when it happens. Mars always has a hidden fury, but when combined with Earth, it triggers the fight or flight response to fight until the death.

In air signs, Mars influences more mental passions rather than physical. It inspires people to learn more and plan their futures. The personality is more likely to become temperamental and will find fault with everything.

When Mars is benefic in your birth chart or an ascendant sign, it means you will become more physically strong and self-confident. It will affect your potential and make you more confident about achieving your goals.

When it is malefic, you will be unable to express your emotions, leading to you becoming shy and introverted. Your sexual needs and your naturally competitive nature will be repressed, leading to you becoming frustrated. These malefic periods allow you the chance to work on these issues and conquer that frustration and become more extroverted. It may not be the best time for you, but Mars is all about challenges and loves it when you find your spirit and work on your personal growth.

The Ancients referred to Mars as the "Lesser Malefic" and credited the planet with accidents, times of crisis, and misfortune.

Mars is sometimes a bully, but he means well. His enthusiasm and ambitious personality mean he will push you even when you are reluctant. In physical terms, he is manifested as a strong young man with an impressive physique and a ruddy complexion. He is choleric and quick to anger but also forgiving.

Deities Relating to Mars

First, let's take a quick look at the Roman god Mars who epitomizes the planet's personality.

He was handsome but vain, and the other gods weren't impressed and disliked him.

His own vanity fooled him into marrying an old and ugly goddess who impersonated the goddess Minerva.

His symbol was a sacred shield

He was the god of soldiers and war

He founded Rome

He was the son of Jupiter and Juno

Other Deities

In Greek Mythology

Ares, the Lord of War and the Inspirer of Daring Deeds, was one of the twelve Olympians and inspired mixed emotions in his followers. They recognized his strength and physical valor, but his passion for brutality and bloodlust made them wary of his power. There are very few temples in his honor compared to his sister Athena who was revered and loved for her strategy and compassion.

Ares was often humiliated by the other gods and was involved in lots of affairs with the wives of other gods. He was referred to as the "*double-faced liar*" and "*the most hated of all Gods*" by Zeus following his poor performance at the battle of Troy.

In Roman Mythology

Mars was often associated with Vulcan, the God of Fire. He allies with the nymphs to combine heat and water to create a protective power against volcanic eruptions and conflagrations. He guards cities and their foodstuffs and is often pictured smelting metals at his sacred furnace.

In Babylonian Mythology

Nusku was the god of volcanoes and was the Exalter of the Sacred Torch. He carried a shining scepter and is pictured bathed in a spiritual light that brings the fire that enlightens the darkness of the human race.

In Hindu Mythology

Agni, a two-faced, seven-armed, three-legged god who rides through the heavens on a ram, is associated with Mars. He breathes fire and uses spiritual axes, spoons, and fans to distribute spiritual libations.

In Egyptian Mythology

Mars is associated with the hawk-headed God Horus of Edfu. He is responsible for keeping the chains of darkness in place and is also the Lord of the Forge. He is ferocious in battle and wears a double-aspect crown that combines the realms of Upper and Lower Egypt, and he sports a kilt and battle gear.

In Celtic Mythology

The Celts admired warriors, and Mars is representative of the most successful yet brutal warrior personalities. Many Celtic deities are associated with him, including Babd, a member of the Morrigan, who were three battle goddesses. She is represented by a raven with a beak that drips blood. Mars also has the same traits as Cocidus, the war god, Medb, the Irish war goddess, and Belatucadros, the British god of destruction.

In Norse Mythology

Mars is associated with Thor, the god of thunder and son of Odin. He is the most barbaric of the Norse gods and rides through the sky with his mighty chariot pulled by goats.

Keywords to Describe the Energy of Mars

- Enthusiasm
- Energy
- Passion

- Anger
- Determination
- Strong-willed
- Stubborn
- Inspiring
- Brave
- Courageous
- Impulsive
- Bullying
- Aggressive
- Leadership
- Action
- Valor
- Conspiracy

Working with Mars

Elemental associations include red crystals and stones like rubies, bloodstone, and garnet. He is strongly associated with iron and metal and is often the dominant sign for metalworkers, blacksmiths, and other careers involving base metal.

Foods include combinations of sour and acrid tastes. Most Mars-dominated signs won't have a sweet tooth. Instead, they prefer more hot and spicy dishes. Garlic, mustard, and peppers will be firm favorites, and alcohol and organic red meats will increase the energies of Mars but may also dull their spiritual intuitions.

Animals Associated with Mars

The Scorpion

Like the planet, you may have a special relationship, but you must always watch out for the sting in the tail. Scorpions are protective and creative but need to be watched just like the energy of Maars.

The Wasp

Another creature that can cause pain with its sting but is also representative of intelligence and teamwork. They work together to create a productive community and have incredible communication skills.

The Ram

Aloof and transformative, the ram has impressive horns to protect his family. They are both aggressive and sensitive, with a sense of vision that exceeds his normal expectations.

The Ox

Strength and loyalty are his traits, and he has grounded energy that exudes his size and power.

The Horse

His innate sense of freedom and adventure sums up the energy of Mars, while his friendship and loyalty show his more compassionate side. Horses are all about mobility and independence and signify your intentions to break free from a boring routine.

The Wolf

Mars is a strong partner to have, as is the wolf. He works well alone or as a pack animal and will stay by your side when you need him. He has a compassionate spiritual side that works well when combined with protective instincts.

Working with Mars in Rituals and Spells

The Tablet of Mars

A table of numbers that contains five rows of five numbers that all add up to sixty-five and totals three hundred and twenty-five is a sacred text used to protect the power of Mars. Use it to make your home safer or to bless your sacred tools. When engraved into the metal, it gives men the potency to win battles and cast out their enemies. It drives away venomous beasts and strikes terror into potential enemies.

Powerful Spells to Win Arguments or Legal Battles

Mars is all about standing your ground and winning battles, but that doesn't always involve physical combat. In modern society, many of our battles are legal or involve documents. Invoke the power of Mars with these potent spells to help you emerge victorious in legal or business matters.

Spell One of the Candle Magick Spells
What You Need:
- Two bay leaves
- Two red candles
- Raw honey
- Copies of the documents relating to your issue
- A lighter
- Gold ribbon

Instructions:
1. Take the candles and coat them with honey.
2. Place them in holders and light them while speaking the following phrase:

   "By the power of Mars, I ask for your help, make my troubles disappear and my future successful. Free me from the trials and tribulations that follow me."
3. Now place the two bay leaves on the documents and tie them with the golden ribbon to form an envelope.
4. Seal the edges with the wax from the candles and state your desired outcome.

Spell Two, the Vinegar Spell for Justice
What You Need:
- A piece of paper
- A red and black pen
- One red candle
- White vinegar
- Fireproof dish

Instructions:
1. When you have a dispute or legal matter, it is essential to share both sides of the story. Write on the paper with the black pen what the issues are and what you have been accused of. Include any slander or false accusations and any that may have a ring of truth.
2. Now turn the paper over and write your truth with the red pen— the whole truth and nothing but the truth, to paraphrase the legal

jargon. Be sincere about all that has happened and show remorse when needed.

3. Pour some of the vinegar onto your hands as you say the following:

    "Mars the mighty leader, I ask for your help to get the truth and justice I seek. Be the power behind my fight and help me to emerge victoriously."

4. Hold the paper in your hands until the vinegar is absorbed, and then light it with the lighter. Let the ashes fall into the fireproof dish until the paper has burned completely. Spread the ashes on the ground outside or under your favorite tree.

5. These spells should be effective for a whole calendar month. If your issue, court case, or argument lasts longer than this, remember to repeat the spells to make sure they are still effective.

The Perfect Ritual to Attract the Power of Mars

Tuesday is the perfect day to connect to the planet Mars, and this is a simple ritual to perform that will connect you to his courage and strength.

What You Need:

- One red pillar candle
- Fancy black iron candle holder
- A black nail used to carve into the candle
- Mars-associated stones like ruby, garnet, or bloodstone
- Allspice
- Cinnamon
- Garlic
- Mustard seeds
- Lighter
- A flat altar or table to perform the ritual
- Red decorations

Instructions:

1. Prepare your altar with your red decorations and make it feel warm and attractive. Place the candelabra on the table so you can access it easily.

2. Engrave the candle with your name and what you want to achieve. Use symbols or single words to avoid confusion. Carve a hole in

the middle of the candle and sprinkle some of your spices into it before spreading the wax to make them secure.

3. Use the rest of the spices to decorate the base of the candle holder to protect your work. Light the candle and watch the wax roll down the pillar and pool on your holder as you repeat the following phrase:

"Lord Mars, I welcome you to my sacred place and grant me the power to live a life filled with courage and passion.

Help me fight my battles with passion and kindness, be they great or small, and help me protect my virtue and reputation.

Draw success to my home and deflect harm and dread. Candle burns, and spirits spin; I ask this ritual magick to begin."

4. The candle needs to be burned down completely, which may take several days. Make sure that number is odd rather than even, so take three, five, or seven days depending on how long you can watch the candle daily.

5. Every time you relight the candle, say, *"As the candle does relight, make my magick reignite."*

Create a Filter for Courage

Filters are a magick potion, and this certain philter is designed to attract the energy of Mars to bring courage to your work. Create the potion on Tuesdays for extra strength and use it whenever you need to add the power of Mars to your magick.

What You Need:

- Red glass bottle
- 2 cups of carrier oil like almond or olive oil
- Eyedropper
- Citrus essential oil
- Black pepper essential oil
- Ginger oil
- Cinnamon
- Dried holly leaf ground into powder
- Fresh basil leaves
- A chip of red garnet or bloodstone

- One red ribbon and one black ribbon
- A small eye of Horus talisman

Instructions:

1. Add the base oil to the bottle, and then use the dropper to add the essential oils.

2. Let your instincts guide you, and add the amounts you feel are appropriate for your potion.

3. Add the chip of stone and the other fresh ingredients.

4. Seal the bottle and shake it gently before you hold it up to the sunshine of the day.

5. Clean the outside of the bottle and tie the ribbons to the neck.

6. Attach the talisman and label it if you have more than one philter in your magick store.

7. Now hold the bottle and visualize how you will use your new powers to improve your life and make yourself more successful. Picture it in your mind's eye and visualize it flowing into the bottle.

8. Repeat these words to make the potion fill with energy

   "This Tuesday philter is my own

   It brings me strength and power,

   I am strong and brave and will not back down

   No person shall steal my hour."

9. Now clean your area and yourself before storing the philter in a dark, cool spot.

10. Take a walk-in nature to ground yourself and reconnect to the earthly plane.

11. Bring the filter out of storage whenever you need the power of Mars and his courage.

Chapter 7: Venus, Love, and Luxury

The mention of Venus conjures up images of love, passion, desire, and beauty. The planet is the second one from the Sun and is roughly the same size as the Earth. It is the brightest planet in our solar system, apart from the Moon and the Sun, and is often referred to as the Morning Star. The planet's surface is completely different from the Earth and is quite hostile, with no oceans and a heavy atmosphere composed of carbon dioxide with virtually no moisture content.

The glyph for Venus is the circle of spirit topping the cross of self which represents the true union of body and mind. Venus is the planet of true love and the potential union of the soul.

> In exaltation, it is in Pisces
>
> In detriment Aries
>
> In dignity, Taurus and Libra
>
> In fall Virgo

Venus is less concentrated on physical passion, which is the domain of Mars, and is more associated with harmony, love, sociability, and a balanced romantic relationship.

Venus in Benefic

When Venus is benefic in a person's house, it indicates wealth, success, and influential positions in society. You will most likely have progressed from lowly beginnings to greater things and enjoy a level of success in your field. Film stars, musicians, designers, models, and charismatic leaders will often have Venus in a benefic position.

They will often have their attention focused on themselves and will tend to forget birthdays, anniversaries, or other occasions that don't feature them. Their relatives and friends will feel ignored and left behind as they become more successful. Even their spouses and children can't change them, and they lack common moral values.

They place a high value on punctuality and expect others to do the same. They will profess to be spiritual and preach to others, but they are materialistic and focused on personal wealth and acquisitions.

Venus in Malefic

When Venus is malefic in a person's house, they will be comfortable but fail to succeed. They will cut ties with their family history and become more focused on their present existence as they get older. Their talents include counterfeiting and creating content for others. They will always earn enough to get by but will never be filled with ambition.

Addiction and excess will always be part of their lives, and they will often fail to sustain successful relationships. They are lazy and irresponsible, but they still command respect from their children, who love them irrespectively.

Venus is also linked with extreme energy, which can cause disasters, and the ancients often sacrificed humans to appease her fury. They believed that when she was angry and her heart was broken, she caused Earthly floods and lightning, which were said to split mountains and create firebrands to terrorize the highlands.

Deities Connected to Venus

In Greek Mythology

Aphrodite is perhaps the most famous goddess associated with Venus. She was reportedly born in Paphos on the island of Cyprus and emerged from the frothy foam of the azure waters where Cronus threw the genitals of his slain father, Uranus. Her romantic and sexual partners included gods and mortals, and her beauty was so impressive it sparked a war amongst the gods.

She was forced into a marriage with the ugly deformed god Hephaestus but had her children with many lovers, including Ares, Poseidon, Adonis, and Hermes. She was the goddess of beauty and fertility and was considered one of the most powerful goddesses in Greek mythology.

In Babylonian Mythology

Inanna was the foremost goddess in Sumerian religion, and she represented both love and war. The goddess appeared in many myths associated with Mesopotamia and was reportedly the goddess who brought culture to society. Inanna is depicted as a beautiful young woman who recognizes her power lies in her appearance and intelligence, yet she was never a faithful wife or mother. Her energy is more associated with early femininity, which takes lovers at will and is fierce and courageous.

In Egyptian Mythology

Isis was a major goddess in ancient Egypt but was often pictured as a human. Her role as a wife and mother made her more accessible than some other goddesses, and she was the grieving widow of the god Osiris. Her intelligence and power of communication meant she was considered more powerful than a thousand soldiers.

The cult of Isis spread throughout Europe, and Romans worshiped her until Emperor Augustus banned the practice as part of his attempt to persuade the Romans to follow Roman Gods. Many pagan traditions have resurrected her to become their patron goddess and home her fecundity and knowledge in modern times.

In Norse Mythology

Frigg is the wife of Odin and the most revered goddess of the Aesir. She represents the most feminine aspects of magick like the hearth, motherhood, love, and the domestic arts. Her motherly love was renowned, and adoring females surrounded her as she held court. Frigg rode through the night on a magnificent chariot pulled by cats, and she was renowned for unlocking lands that had previously remained unexplored.

Her symbols include the spinning wheel and mistletoe, and she represents the ultimate mother figure. She tried to save her son's life by altering fate but could not keep him from an untimely death. Known as the mother of Asgard, she has strong links with the Roman deity Venus.

Elements of Venus

She is linked to the colors Green, pink, rose, white, turquoise, purple, blue, and silver.

Crystals Associated with Venus

Calcite: The stone responsible for doubling the energy and amplifying confidence. It is considered a multivitamin for the soul and will help you increase vigor and vitality. Use it to connect to the hedonistic part of your personality and increase your desire for life and all it can give you.

Celestite: Use this crystal to calm yourself when facing stress and calamity. It connects directly to the energy of Venus when used in rituals and brings her female nurturing quality to your work. It has a high vibration that will bring peace and calm to the most troubling situations.

Emerald: The stone of success in love and romance, the emerald also enhances other relationships. It can be given as a gift to cement platonic friendships, or it can be used to strengthen self-love and confidence. Use it to improve your emotional understanding of yourself and start on the path of self-discovery.

Green Tourmaline: A powerful healing stone linked to the Heart Chakra. It has masculine energy to heal your physical wounds and strong feminine energy to bring relief to your emotional and spiritual scars.

Malachite: A powerful stone that resonates with the female aspects of health. It can help you balance any issues in the reproductive system or bring relief to menstrual trauma. Use it to channel the energy of Venus to cure your ills or just strengthen your internal organs.

Keywords Used to Describe the Energy of Venus

- Affinity
- Love
- Passion
- Desire
- Lust
- Beauty

- Attraction
- Wanton desire
- Femininity
- Vanity
- Self-obsession
- Satisfaction
- Ambition
- Family ties
- Female energy
- Self-image
- Eroticism
- Adventurousness
- Intimacy
- Jealousy
- Relationships
- Complicity

Spirit Animals Connected to Venus

The Elephant

Strong, magnificent, and dignified. Female elephants are renowned for their mothering skills, and herds of elephants protect their young fiercely. The elephant is part of the royal family of nature and is regal yet approachable.

The Dove

The symbol of peace and tranquility, the dove, may not seem a natural choice for Venus. However, it symbolizes the love and devotion you hope will be part of your relationships and inspires you to sacrifice your ego to attain the perfect union. They are the symbol of communication and gentleness.

The Peacock

With its bright plumage and immense sense of self-love, the peacock is the perfect representation of the energy of Venus. It displays itself to attract love and isn't afraid to show its intentions. If you find yourself drawn to the peacock, you need to work on your self-esteem and be more receptive to love and attraction.

The Sheep

If you find yourself in tune with sheep, it means you are more likely to be drawn to compassionate relationships instead of passionate ones. You are attracted by levelheaded personalities and want to avoid drama or turmoil.

The Goat

Strong and vigorous, the goat symbolizes strength both physically and emotionally. They work well alone and aren't afraid to butt heads to get what they want.

Foods Associated with Venus

Although most people with Venus strong in their house will have a sweet tooth, they love to combine that sweetness with an acidic or astringent partner. Sweet and sour chicken or honey and mustard combinations will appeal to their pallet. They love candies and dried fruits and can tend to overindulge in their favorite foods. Sweet wine and liquors are high on their treat lists, and they will often combine this with salty snacks. Foods spiced with essential oils are also tempting, and the addition of fennel, mint, basil, or vanilla makes their dishes more appealing.

Venus is associated with fragrances like honeysuckle, jasmine, lilac, myrtle, and other feminine scents, and they will often use essential oils and diffusers in the home. Think feminine, and you will get the essence of Venus.

Love Spells through the Planet Venus

Love isn't just about bumping genitals with your partner, although it is pleasurable. True love is about embracing all things luxurious, opulent, splendid, and magnificent. It's about eating the finest foods and experiencing the softest and most comfortable fabrics while you bask in luxurious surroundings.

Nobody is promising that your life will suddenly become one filled with jewels, sportscars, and houses straight out of a magazine. You can expect to attract a better style of living and gain the skills to appreciate what you are given. Love is about happiness, filling your wildest desires, and becoming accustomed to pleasure.

Invoking the goddess Venus and the energy she brings is like gaining a VIP pass to life. Ask her to join you and help you become connected to her feminine wiles and the strength they incur.

Invoke the goddess and the planet of Venus by the following methods:

- Dress to impress: Strut your stuff in a FABULOUS outfit that screams "Look at me NOW" to show your intention.
- Create a sacred space with roses, sweet honey, your favorite candies, crystals, and a red, pink, and white candle.
- Take a ritual bath with your favorite essential oils and float rose petals in the water. Choose your softest pink or white towels to dry off with, and use scented creams to feel special.
- Draws a circle with pink or red chalk and ask her in.

Create a Simple Love Scent Filled with the Power of Venus

Perfumes and scents attract us. The smell of something pleasant and attractive can stop you in your tracks. Create a low-level scent to make the first move in contacting someone you are interested in.

What you need:

- Four drops of rose oil
- One drop of lavender oil
- One drop of myrrh oil
- One drop of sandalwood oil
- One drop of ylang-ylang oil
- Twenty drops of carrier oil like olive or almond oil

Instructions:

Mix thoroughly and apply sparingly to your skin when you are in the presence of someone you want to attract. If they are receptive to your intent, it will cause them to respond. If they have no attraction to you at all, even the most powerful potion won't work.

Candle Spells for Love

Candles are very effective for love magick, and they are available in many styles, colors, and shapes. Depending on your intentions, here are some of the more effective ways to use candles in your magick work.

Image candles have been used for generations to represent intentions in magick. Male and female candles are the most obvious type of images, but other powerful kinds can be used. We will start with ordinary candles for our love spells and discover how to carve them to represent two parts of a couple.

Love Spells with Candles

Choose two candles to represent yourself and the object of your affection. These can be as simple as pink, white, or black candles, or you can choose colors that represent your individual energies. Green, red, yellow, and orange candles work just as effectively.

Write the name of the two parties on the candles that represent them and anoint the separate candles with oil.

Place the two candles on an altar or suitable workspace and place a red candle between the two. Light all three candles and move the two image candles closer to the red candle as you visualize the union they will form.

Once the two image candles are attached to the red candle, continue to watch them burn as you think about the object of your affection and your future. Once the candles have burned down, take the wax, and bury it in the garden.

Spell for Marriage Commitment

If you are already in a committed relationship, this spell will help you strengthen the bonds and make your union stronger.

Take two candles representing you and your partner and add your individual perfumes or scents to them to anoint the candles. Place a photo of yourselves in front of your candles and tie the two together with a red ribbon.

Light the candles and say the following:

"I light the flames of love and ask that the goddess Venus helps us stay together with the light of her love. Keep the fire of love burning in our home for as long as her bright planet shines from the heavens."

Let the candles burn to the point where the ribbon binds them before extinguishing the flames. Take the two candles and keep them somewhere safe. If you need to strengthen the spell in the future, just move the ribbon lower and repeat the spell.

There are other types of spells you can cast with candles. Everybody knows that love can end just as quickly as it begins and that most of us will experience at least one breakup in our lives and need to move on. Love and romance are transient, and sometimes we all need a helping hand moving forward.

Spells for breakups are cast by using the two image candles in the same way as in love spells, but they move away from each other in these instances. Place the image candles on an altar or a flat surface ad tie them with the red ribbon-like before. Light them and remove the ribbon while making them move away from each other.

Say:

"We part as friends and with love rather than hate, Venus bless us both and seal our fate, we lived as one but now that time is done."

As the two candles burn down, imagine how you will face the future alone and experience adventures as a single person.

Take the wax remains and bury them separately in the ground.

Commercial Image Candles

As magick and spiritual workings become more popular, sources of image candles have increased. You can purchase specific candles to make your work more structured and effectively signal your intentions.

Bride and groom candles can be purchased that look like wedding cake toppers. Black candles should signal the end of a relationship, while white ones are used to encourage love or attract a proposal. Red marriage candles used with these image candles will make your spells attract passion, love, and vitality to your relationships.

Hugging candles are dual wicked and depict a couple in an embrace. They can be used to attract love back to you who has left the relationship or strengthen your bonds. Your words and intent will determine the efficiency of the spell you cast. These candles are mostly available in pink and red and are a source of positive energy.

Image candles help you focus your spells and bring your intentions to the front of your spell. Use the colors and images with the strength of conviction to make your work more powerful. You have the resources, so make sure you utilize them.

Candle Colors and Their Meaning

- Red is the color of passion and pace. Use red to make your intentions happen sooner and attract passion and sex to your magick.

- Green is the color of prosperity and luck. Use it to add money and wealth to your spells.

- Pink is the gentle energy of happiness, romance, purity, and new relationships. It is used to bring tenderness and spiritual satisfaction to your work and to calm the emotions after a dispute.

- Black candles signal the end of something. Just like Venus was the bringer of love, she was also associated with death. Black candles are used to help you focus on new things and leave the past behind.

Other Image Candles You Can Use

- Skull candles can look menacing, but they are effective for reading people's minds. Use them to bring protection and heal illnesses or deal with pain. Skulls are effective in bringing protection and change to your life.

- Cat candles bring good luck to your magick. They also attract the energy of Venus through their association with Frigg and her magnificent cat-drawn chariot.

- Seven knob candles are designed to make daily spells more effective. They represent the seven days of the week, and you should use the knobs individually or together, depending on your needs. Carve intentions and needs into the candles and light them on a required day.

Chapter 8: Jupiter, Expand your Resources

Venus may have tended to your emotional needs, but now it's time to seek help with your exuberance and expansion. Prosperity and wealth are in your sights, and Jupiter will help you. He is the King of the Planets and the largest planet in the solar system. Jupiter was the King of the Gods in Roman mythology, and all prayers passed through him. He rules the skies with divine authority and is responsible for the underworld.

Jupiter's glyph is a crescent connected to the light of the matter. Modern interpretations include a representation of the number 24, which signifies energy that is available whenever you need it.

He has wise energy and is of the utmost authority. His rule is fair, expansive, and open-minded. Jupiter has proud and arrogant energy, but he will advise you with wisdom and pride. If Jupiter is present in your sign, it means he can help you with your astral growth to discover your potential. He will encourage you to grow and highlight the positive parts of your personality.

Jupiter in water element signs will encourage you to build relationships and learn from new experiences. He will show you ways to become more creative and imaginative.

In fire element signs, he will stimulate your ambitions and encourage you to seek promotion or break free and become your own boss. He brings good luck in challenges and will make you confident to try new things.

Earth element signs provoke you to change traditional rules and buck the trend. Don't follow like sheep; become someone who questions rules and challenges authority. Jupiter will also push you to get what you want, materially and spiritually. Raise your standard of living and enjoy the fruits of your labor.

In air element signs, it helps you expand your horizons and learn new stuff. Think outside of the box and choose activities and social events that are novel and interesting. Jupiter will also encourage you to help others and try charity work or volunteering.

Jupiter in Benefic

People with Jupiter in the benefic will often be educated to a higher level and will be skilled in their chosen profession. They are mentors and have a helpful nature. They offer advice but then stand back to let the other person make their own decisions.

They avoid controversy, and even if they are in a position to help close friends or family, they will only do so if the rules allow it. They won't break conventional barriers for anyone. If someone challenges them and opposes their views, they are enemies from that day forward.

They will always find a way to make money and live comfortable lives. Their relatives will see them as a financial source butt will rarely be allowed to take advantage of them. They are effective communicators, but a lack of tact will make their behavior controversial.

Jupiter in Malefic

They may be physically attractive, but their individual style doesn't look good on everyone. They have high positions but are base thinkers with low morals and often abuse their position.

Even if they have millions in the bank, they still feel the need for even more and will lie and cheat to get just a few more bucks. They don't believe in charity but will donate if it makes them look good to the public. They can't be trusted with secrets and will trade your trust to gain other people's favor.

They don't trust the media and believe that all journalists and pundits are out to get them. They will appoint someone to a position at work and then appoint another person to spy on them. They don't trust anyone and are constantly looking over their shoulder.

In family matters, they believe that male children are more important than females and will argue the point with other female family members. They will change their social contacts in a heartbeat if it means their new friends will help them progress.

Never take a loan from them, as they will constantly refer to the fact until you repay the debt. They also refuse to collect money relating to spiritual causes or religious institutions.

Jupiter is in exaltation in Cancer

In detriment in Gemini

In dignity in Sagittarius and Pisces

In fall in Capricorn

Deities Associated with Jupiter

Jupiter is the Roman god of the Pantheon and the god of light who concentrated on helping the ancient people to work out their connections to the light and nature on Earth.

He was known as the god of rain when using the name Pluvius and the god of truth with the name Fulger. He also represented thunder with the epithet Fulger.

Jupiter was one of six siblings fathered by Saturn. His father swallowed all five children born before Jupiter, and his mother moved the baby to protect him. When he grew up, he forced his father to vomit all the children, joining Jupiter to overthrow his father.

In Greek Mythology

The oldest and most revered god in Greek mythology, Zeus, is the father of the gods and was famed for his erotic affairs, which resulted in multiple offspring. He was notoriously unfaithful to his wife and cheated on her repeatedly.

In mythology, he is pictured with a thunderbolt in one hand and a scepter in the other. He governs the weather and is often accompanied by a giant golden eagle named Aetos Dios, who helps him rule the heavens.

Zeus is an arbitrary god and has two urns. One is filled with blessings and the other with afflictions. He bestows them on mortals depending on their behavior and whether they have pleased or offended him. He is a warrior and a savior to his followers and is the keeper of oaths.

In Egyptian Mythology

Amun-Ra is the most powerful deity in Egyptian mythology, and his name means the creator of all things. He created himself and then gave birth to the rest of the universe. He was considered omnipresent and honored as the god of gods.

In Norse Mythology

Odin was the equivalent of Jupiter and was known for his wisdom and strength. He ruled with a fair and balanced hand, but he still inspired frenzy and rage. He was constantly seeking knowledge and would sacrifice himself to understand the universe's secrets.

In Indian Mythology

Lakshmi is the goddess of wealth and prosperity. She is often pictured with the god Vishnu and was believed to act as his special envoy. She is wise and fertile and represents the Trivedi, the most powerful trio of Indian goddesses.

Keywords in Jupiter Magick

- Expansion
- Growth
- Luck
- Good fortune
- Ritual
- Freedom
- Generosity
- Luxury
- Opulence
- Success
- Philosophy
- Knowledge
- Learning
- Faith

Jupiter is associated with the colors purple, sage, turquoise, blue, deep green, and yellow.

Gemstones and crystals include amethyst, lapis lazuli, sodalite, emeralds, moonstone, selenite, and carnelian.

Food That Appeals to Jupiter

Jupiter people love oily tastes, such as pistachios.
https://unsplash.com/photos/b6bizty3pz8?utm_source=unsplash&utm_medium=referral&utm_content=creditShareLink

Jupiter people love oily and sweet tastes. If Jupiter is dominant in your sign, it means you will be drawn to sweets that are also savory, like Indian arisa putha, which are deep-fried and include jaggery and rice flour. Pistachios and ghee will also feature in your diet. Wheat and barley are your staple ingredients and favorite foods to help build your strength and provide a tonic for your system.

Spirit Animals Relating to Jupiter

The Cheetah

With quick thinking and passionate movements, the cheetah represents freedom and exploration. He moves with certainty and is a skilled hunter and protector of his family.

The Bull

Steadfast and courageous, the masculine energy promotes wealth and prosperity and is part of Jupiter's band of animals. If you dream of bulls, you are competitive and seek good times. If you are eating a bull, you need to address your difficulties and solve disputes. If you are riding the bull, you will be successful in business or career matters.

The Dragon

This mythical creature represents transformation and motivation. They are filled with inspirational energy and bring protection and authority to your life. If you dream of dragons, you will be successful and attract prosperity.

The Eagle

They are goal orientated and know how to soar above the earth. They have an advanced vision and represent the freedom of Jupiter and his energy. Dreaming of eagles signifies you are ready to spread your wings and find new projects.

Jupiter and Travel

Jupiter is the planet of positivity and appeals to a strong sense of discovery. It encourages people to travel far beyond the normal tourist spots. People with strong connections to Jupiter will travel for education rather than entertainment. They will favor trips that take them into undiscovered societies and civilizations so they can learn from their cultures. You won't find Jupiter-influenced signs at the beach, or if you do, it will be the coolest, most remote beach ever.

Negative Aspects of Jupiter Energies

When you have this planet on your side, you will tend to believe that success comes easily, leading to complacency. Natural achievements and good luck will only take you so far, and you risk becoming lazy. They strongly believe that they are superior and way beyond other mere mortals, which can be perceived as arrogance and dismissiveness.

Guided Meditation to Invoke the Power of Jupiter

When you have a strong Jupiter alliance, you find it hard to sleep and will often be so caught up in your thoughts that it's hard to switch off. This meditation isn't strictly astrologically centered on Jupiter but is a more generic exercise that will help you drift off.

Bring yourself to the present moment by sitting in a quiet place free from distractions and choosing a comfortable position. Concentrate your mind by tracing your middle finger along the contours of your face and the neck curve until you find your mind is still and ready to concentrate.

Repeat the exercise so you become even more relaxed, but let your finger travel along your body this time. Be aware of the ground's firmness o and feel as light as a cloud between your feet and the top of your head.

Touch your forehead and bless your thoughts.

Touch your mouth gently and bless your words.

Begin to take a deep breath as your finger travels to your ribcage and feel it elevate. Let your breath free the upper half of your body as you begin the journey to your hip bones. Imagine two screws holding your hips in place and unscrewing them to let your body free.

Continue down your legs until your reach the thighs, knees, and toes. As you unlock that final pinky, you will feel yourself fly and embrace the freedom. You are now ready for sleep and will feel relaxed and ready for your night's rest.

Money and Prosperity Spells

Jupiter's energy is prominent on Thursdays and will help you gain success in financial and prosperity matters. Its energy can help you in the following spells and is especially strong 208 days after your birthday.

The Wallet Spell

Choose a red wallet for your spell and place a small mirror between the banknotes inside it. This will help you mirror the money and make it double. Bless the wallet with this phrase *"I keep my cash in this ruby red case to make it increase; with Jupiter's help, my work will never cease."*

Never leave a wallet empty when it has a mirror in it, as this will cause you a lack of luck and prosperity.

Speak to Your Money

Everyone knows that communication is the key to a great relationship, so why would your relationship with your financial self be any different? It is considered crass and taboo to talk freely about money, so do something typically Jupiter-based and break this social barrier. Talk to your friends about financial matters and praise successful and wealthy people. Encourage them to become more fiscally interested and seek financial independence. Remember that envy and jealousy won't help you. Speak with love, respect, and positivity, and you will benefit from Jupiter's energy.

Now speak directly to your money and share your thoughts, hopes, and aspirations with actual physical representations of money. Take the notes from your wallet or purse and chat to them about how they can work for you. Talking freely to them as if they were your friends will help you change your attitude toward wealth. Break those taboos and talk to your cash.

Shimmering Silver Spell

Prosperity spells work, but they don't encourage greed. Use this spell when you need a bit more cash but not to make you rich. Use the Jupiter glyph or crystals to boost the spell and make it more intense.

What You Need:

- A bowl or cauldron
- Fresh mint leaves
- Freshwater
- A silver coin

Instructions:

1. Place the coin (an old dime works well) at the bottom of the bowl and add the water.

2. Drop the mint leaves into the bowl while repeating this phrase

   "Jupiter, the stars and moon, come to me and bless me soon, as the light makes silver shine, use your power to make wealth mine."

3. Leave the bowl in the moonlight overnight, and then take the coin out. Carry it with you for good luck.

Prosperity Spell
What You Need:

- Green candle
- Black pepper oil
- Vanilla oil
- Silver coin
- Sharp pencil

1. Anoint the candles and use the pencil to carve the word "wealth" along the candle. If you have a specific request, add that as well.
2. Place the coin in a candle holder and put the candle on top.
3. Light it and let it burn down completely and when you have the wax-covered coin, place it in a safe place to help you attract wealth and prosperity.

Chapter 9: Saturn – Manifest Your Destiny

Saturn is the furthest planet from the Sun and is often depicted as an older man in astrological and magic terms. The masculine energy he brings is concerned with Saturn is referred to as Chronos and has the epithet "The Father of Time." Your magickal connection will help you deal with financial aspects of the future and how to gain knowledge of what lies ahead for you in all parts of your life.

The most remote planet in the solar system, Saturn is a slow-moving yet serious energy source. It brings patience and balance to the mix and is instrumental in promoting caution where some of the other planets will tell you to jump right in. It is in opposition to the Sun and Moon, and in traditional astronomy, it was regarded as a negative planet. In more modern terms, it is recognized that caution can sometimes be the more sensible attitude, and Saturn is regarded as a great leveling energy that makes us think twice.

The glyph of Saturn is the cross of matter with a right-sided hook that looks like the letter h and represents the weight of responsibility that humans carry throughout their lives.

> Saturn is in exaltation in Libra
>
> In detriment in Cancer
>
> In dignity in Capricorn and Aquarius
>
> In fall in Aries

Saturn in malefic and benefic in your horoscope

When Saturn is in the malefic, it brings creation, unusual talents, and successful management skills. They will be sought out to give advice and a shoulder to cry on. They will help their friends and relatives even if they will have to sacrifice their possessions or emotions, but they won't be appreciated.

They have hidden talents and won't become successful early in life. They will be more likely to come into their own in middle age or even when they retire. They will be close to their parents and will often still live at home even though they have the means to move out. Their lives will be focused on work which means they won't have the same relationship with their children as they have with their parents.

Blessed with a strong sense of self-belief, they will argue the point when they believe they are right, and because some people are frightened of them, they won't hear the truth from others. People will find it easier to agree and move on rather than attract the anger they may face when they disagree with them.

They will be successful in most fields but will likely lose money in property deals. They will be attracted to careers in banking, construction, undertaking, teaching, and history, where they will always give 110% to their work and neglect their social life and family.

Saturn in Benefic

They are very single-minded, which means they are great researchers. They complicate things and turn simple obstacles into major stress indicators. Most of them will be servants of humanity and dedicate their lives to finding cures for the world's ills. They refuse to put themselves and their family first and will often let their finances suffer for the good of others.

Despite this, their family and friends understand what drives them and are forgiving and loving toward them. They have strong family ties and a fixed sense of morals. Working towards high standards, they set themselves a strict code to live by and are opposed to corruption and injustice.

People with Saturn in the benefic are dedicated to solving race, discrimination, and any bias in the world. Their love of animals and wildlife will be evident, and their overall compassion and discipline will set a good example for future generations.

When aligned to water signs, it signals a tendency to hold grudges and self-isolate. They refuse to heal emotionally and would rather dwell in the past than move on.

In fire signs, it limits pleasurable activities by focusing on more rigid beliefs. It promotes sacrifice and self-limiting to give more time to charity and worthy pastimes than those more self-centered.

In earth signs, it signals caution. People in this category are not groundbreakers, and they prefer to let other people take risks while sticking to traditional methods and beliefs.

Deities Associated with Saturn

In Roman mythology, Saturn was the god of agriculture and was responsible for teaching the ancient Romans how to cultivate grapes and farm the land. He ruled with two faces represented by his two wives. One was named Ops and was the goddess of opulence and plenty, while Lua was the goddess of destruction. Saturn was civilized but had a violent side.

His most famous custom was called Saturnalia and was a week filled with banquets and drinking games. Gladiators would fight, and gifts would be given. Masters and slaves would exchange roles, and it was a time for people to relax and forget about the strict rules of Roman society.

In Greek Mythology

Cronus was the Greek equivalent and was connected to the seasons and time passage. He was the youngest of the Titans, and he sat alone in the Elysian fields. He castrated and overthrew his father, married his sister, and fathered their six children.

In Native American Mythology

Kokopelli was the god of agriculture and was a renowned trickster. He played the flute to herald the end of winter and the beginning of spring.

In Celtic Mythology

Dagda was the god of agriculture and was also depicted playing the harp. He was an older man who was wise and dispensed his wisdom to the Irish people. He was responsible for the year's seasons appearing in the correct order.

In Egyptian Mythology

Neper was the god of the grain, and Nepit was the goddess whose body was marked with dots to represent the corn. They were known as the lord and lady of the mouth to show the importance of grain in feeding humans.

As planet energy goes, Saturn is unique because he represents limitations no matter what the position in the astral plane. He is the solid energy that brings you back to Earth and makes you reassess. His energy is the lodestone of life that makes us into responsible beings and reminds us that other people matter.

Keywords for Saturn

- Limits
- Control
- Forward thinking
- Structure
- Borders
- Conservation
- Strength
- Death
- Wisdom
- Knowledge
- Darkness and light
- Dismissal
- Denial
- Time
- Mentor
- Responsibility
- Self-introspection
- Tools
- Locks
- Cold
- Ice
- Fear

Saturn is the planet of limitations, but it makes us address our finitude. Where would we be if we didn't observe borders and rules? Mars teaches us to fight, and Jupiter brings us luck, but Saturn reigns in our over-enthusiasm and teaches us there is no substitute for hard work and diligence.

Saturn is associated with the colors black, grey, blue, orange, and yellow, representing the lighter side of the planet's psyche.

Gemstones and crystals include black tourmaline, clear quartz, Apache tears, hematite, and obsidian.

Foods Associated with Saturn

Bitter and pungent food appeals to Saturn's energy, and they will eat small meals often rather than large meals at designated mealtimes. Healthy astringent foods like apples, pomegranates, avocado, sprouts, and green bananas will help them avoid fatty foods. They recognize the importance of foods that detoxify the body and blood and will include spinach, herbal teas, lemon, and turmeric in their dishes to make them tasty and healthy.

Spirit Animals Related to Saturn

The Dog

Loyal and brave, dogs represent the steadfast part of Saturn's energy. They are protective and patient, but they also give love unconditionally.

The Falcon

Falcons have perfect balance and can see for miles. They represent the foresighted energy of the planet and will bring happiness and clarity to your world.

The Inchworm

This lowly creature is often overlooked, but it is integral to the animal world. Saturn is the patron of all wildlife and salutes even the smallest link. Inchworms are experts at concealment, and they represent transformation and mutation.

The Mouse

Filled with stealth and understanding, the mouse is a signal of having an eye for detail and being grounded. They have a natural modesty and innocence.

The Jellyfish

With complete transparency and intention, the jellyfish is beautiful but can bring pain and sometimes death. Saturn has the same energy with its distinctive shape and hidden depths.

Rituals Invoking Saturn and the Power It Holds

Saturday is the preferred day to perform any Saturn rituals, so try and make time for this powerful way to create a platform of Saturn.

What You Need:

- Six white tealights
- One large black candle
- Incense burner
- Sesame oil
- Essential myrrh oil
- Clear water from a natural source
- Rock salt
- Black rice
- Black mustard seeds
- Lighter
- Small glasses for offerings

Instructions:

1. Take the six tea lights to represent the other planets and place them in a circle with the black candle in the center.

2. Add water to the glasses and put a pinch of the dry ingredients in each.

3. Place the myrrh oil and sesame oil on an incense burner, put it on the right of the black candle, and light it.

4. Use the glasses to form a triangle to the left of the black candle.

5. Light each of the six candles concerning the power they command and the respect you hold for them.

6. Now light the black candle and recite a dedication to Saturn with the following:

"Lord of the seventh heaven, mighty Saturn, I ask that you shine your light into this space. Keep us safe and illuminated with your power, and show us the path to take. Fill our sous with your blessings and help us make decisions that benefit both ourselves and the world."

7. Let the candles burn naturally once you have completed the ritual, and then take a spiritual bath. Cleanse yourself thoroughly and take the wax to the garden to bury it.

Saturn is a complicated energy and prefers that you conduct daily deeds to please him rather than performing more ritualistic displays. He is benevolent and believes in helping others. Here are some ways to appease him and let his energy into your life:

1. **Pay Your Karmic Debts:** Saturn is the lord of karmic debts, and he encourages their repayment. Volunteer or donate your time and money to worthy causes to pay back any karmic mistakes you may have made in former lives. In Sanskrit, these debts are called Danam, and paying them back helps strangers become friends and makes your enemies less hostile.

2. **Share Food with Others on Saturday:** What is better than sitting down with your friends and family sharing a meal? Why not extend that feeling by sharing food with those less fortunate than yourself. Arrange an event in your garden or a local space to feed homeless people or families living on the breadline. Encourage other people to lend a hand and make the event joyful and fulfilling.

3. **Feed the Birds:** Saturn encourages us all to feed the soul, and the body, so make the same dedication to the wildlife. Feeding birds in nature is both pleasurable and worthy.

4. **Spend Saturday Doing Jobs That Need to Be Done:** How often have you put off menial and boring jobs because "it's the weekend" and dedicated the time to more pleasurable jobs. Remember that Saturn represents the work that must be done and the people who must work regardless of the day or time. Join them and spend your free time doing tasks that need to be done.

5. **Get Organized:** Saturn loves discipline, so removing clutter and debris from your life will make your intention to connect to him more apparent. Make a to-do list and start to get your life back on track. Remove mental clutter and physical by removing methods

of communication with people who have no relevance in your life anymore. Yes, that's right, get rid of all of your past partners or friends you may be tempted to reach out to. There's a reason you don't have them in your life, and now is the time to make the break.

6. **Walk Barefoot on the Grass:** Saturn wants us to be humbler and removing your shoes and feeling the grass between your toes is a great start. It shows us that weakness and compliance aren't negative ways of thinking. Grass can't withstand strong storms by staying upright. It knows that the only way to survive is to bend and take shelter until the storm passes. It takes strength from the storm and emerges refreshed and more alive than before. Learn from the grass and know when it is time to bend rather than put your head above the parapet.

Saturn encourages us to take responsibility for our own lives by tracking. If you are overweight and you know it's because you eat too much, start tracking your calories and exercise levels. Are you emotionally drained by the people you have in your life? Track how you feel when you are in their company. Use the results to make changes and become more emotionally responsible. Knowing the problems is the first step toward major changes, and Saturn loves this tracking idea.

Chapter 10: Making a Planetary Altar

Alters will help you focus your intentions.
https://www.pexels.com/photo/a-person-putting-golden-plate-with-food-on-the-altar-8818668/

Working with the planets can be done anywhere. It will produce results, but making an altar will help you focus your intentions and concentrate your efforts by using a designated space to perform your magick. And it looks amazing!

It can be a place for meditation and reflection and an active center for your work. Altars have been used for millennia as sacred places to offer food and perform rites of passage. They give communities a common bond for worship and have evolved from simple wooden structures into more elaborate structures. They represent the seasons, the god or gods worshipped, and often display other representations of the deities and influences.

First, there are no fixed rules for altars. It is your sacred place, so make it relevant to yourself and your beliefs. It shouldn't be an intimidating or stressful endeavor. The process should be joyful and uplifting for your soul and spirit. Make it authentic and choose items that speak to your soul; your sacred space should be a powerful place for you to channel your energy and feel at home.

Choose Your Space

Depending on your available space, this can range from a whole room to a small box. Some people create shoebox-sized altars that can be taken with them and a more fixed space, but as with all things relating to your altar, the choice is yours.

Most people choose a natural surface to form the base of their altars, like a decorative wooden shelf, a stone, or marble, depending on your budget. Some kitchen cutting boards have amazing decorations and are ready-made bases that can be bought from kitchen stores. Remember, the base of your altar will dictate how many items you can place on it and how easy it will be to assemble or disassemble. Make sure the base is at a comfortable height to work on. Some people prefer to work seated, using a lower altar.

Because the work with planets is more effective in natural light, it is better to place your altar near a window or another opening that will allow you to use light to illuminate the surface. The position you place your altar in can link it with the elements. North is connected to the Earth, East to air, South to fire, and West to water. Placing your altar on a movable stand means you can turn it in alternate directions depending on your intentions.

Decorate the Space

You are working with the celestial bodies, so acknowledge that with a planetary-based decoration. There are hundreds of styles to choose from, and you can buy planetary tablecloths, stickers, hanging garlands, and glow-in-the-dark wall art that is both decorative and informative. Luckily the planets appeal to many people, so you can get these items easily and for very little cash. You can also get some effective lighting that projects solar system images onto the walls and ceiling for under $30 on Amazon.

Now choose some items from your home to represent you. You can use a small piece of jewelry or your favorite crystal. Choose objects that mean the world to you to show the planets you are invested in – and that your intentions are strong. If you buy things, especially for the altar, try and choose sustainable items that are good for the planet.

Tools to Have on Your Altar

Depending on your taste, you can choose to pack your altar with tools like:

- Wand – You can make your own or choose one made of your favorite wood to concentrate energy rather than use your fingers or hands

- Besom – A magical broom you can use to clear away negative energies

- Candles

- Cauldron or Bowl - For mixing your potions and making infusions

- Minerals and Crystals – Choose a representative stone for each of the planets so you can use them to concentrate your intent

- Plants and Flowers – Give your altar life with plants that will breathe life into your spells, and flowers symbolize health and vitality

- Mirror – to create light and abundance

- Statues of your favorite deities

- Pentagram

- Objects That Represent the Elements – A jar of water, a candle, a feather, and a pot of earth help you utilize elements in your spells

- Dried herbs

- Essential oils

- Items to Represent Your Desires – Money like coins or bills, healing stones, red hearts for love, or anything else you like.

Get Some Ideas from Other People

There is no reason you can't get inspired by other people's ideas. Pinterest and Instagram have plenty of colorful and inspiring designs. They include pagan and Wiccan altars, which are designed to be used indoors and outdoors. Why not use your space outside to create a natural shrine to the planets and welcome their energy?

Use bowls to represent the four elements and fill them with corresponding items. This helps you to move them when needed to come to the front of the altar when they are included in a certain spell. Your altar should be beautiful and feel like home. When you achieve that level of love and satisfaction, your altar is fit for purpose.

Assemble your altar and use it. The more you use your sacred space, the more effective it becomes. Don't restrict your space to just magic work. Use it to meditate and practice yoga. Sit in your space and write a journal or read quietly, surrounded by the planet's love. Make your time there special, and don't use it for storage or as a dumping ground. Keep it free from clutter and let the natural energies flow freely. Clutter and detritus will stop it from being effective.

Clean Your Altar Regularly

Your altar is your temple so treat it with respect and love. Don't neglect it, and make sure you lavish your love and attention on it. Cleanse it regularly with salt and water to purify the space and banish negative energy. Cleanse the area with sage and incense and make it appealing to your soul.

Bring gifts and offerings to the planets like food and drink. Bring crystals and other stones to decorate and make your space special. Make the space a higher representation of your true self and regularly show it love and respect. Some people like to start their day with time spent at their altar and then finish the day in the same place. It helps you become grounded and concentrated in the morning and helps you destress before bedtime.

Key Points to Remember

- Your altar should be in a place you can keep safe and free from negative energies
- Rely on your intuition to decide what is included
- It should be fun and filled with joy

- Items on the altar should evolve as you do
- It should make you feel special
- You want to spend time there
- It is a constant reminder of your desires and goals
- It helps you direct and channels your energy

Portable Altars

During the First World War, military chaplains were appointed for the soldiers' needs on the battlefield. The unique situation created by the combatants meant that Christians were killing other Christians en masse, and the need for their services increased. All military corps had chaplains, and their altars are available to view in museums.

Your portable altar should be light, portable, and suited to your needs. It may be the size of a briefcase or as small as a box you can carry in your pocket. You may prefer a bag to carry your altar components so it can double as an altar cloth or a box that has a design on the lid.

Try and include elements of the planets. A small twig, a flat stone, or a vial of salt for the Earth, or you can carry a small pentacle.

Air can be represented by a feather, a small wand, or an incense stick.

Fire can be represented by a single match or a lighter.

Water can be represented by a vial of liquid or a seashell.

Add some small crystals and herbs to your altar, and include your favorite items on your altar. The smallest container can be used as a portable altar, it represents your intentions, and that's what matters.

You can buy a kit-like altar that already contains sprays, altar cloth, crystals, and incense if you prefer. They give you the chance to create a Zen space to practice your planetary divinations.

Bonus 7-Day Guide to Connect to the Planets

We already know how the planets are related to the days of the week and that the modern names of days often come directly from the name of the planet it aligns with. Using these connections helps you form a stronger bond with the astral powers and brings a daily form of magic to your regular routines.

Use these cosmic themes combined with what you already know about the planets to make each day special and use the energy it creates naturally to fit into your schedule.

Monday

The day of the Moon and the start of most people's working week is often described as manic and stressful. Because it is a day to start work, it can be frenzied and full of emotional pitfalls. The Moon is a feminine and emotionally charged planet, and it will affect your moods. Do everything you can to become mindful of her energy and use it to make your day more fulfilling and less draining.

Clothing

Wear white when you can and avoid energy-draining colors. Remember that the Moon is often associated with triple female deities, so try changing your outfit to reflect this. Honor the maiden by wearing fun jewelry or accessories even when you must dress conservatively.

Foods

Be careful what you eat, as the Moon will affect your digestion. Monday is not the time to try new foods as the Moon rules your body and is used to certain tastes.

Meditate in the Morning

Take ten minutes to ground your energy at your altar or in your garden. Sit on a cushion and close your eyes before breathing deeply and holding your breath. Take this time to reflect on what you want from the day ahead and visualize how you will progress. Let your breath out slowly and ask the Moon to shine on you today.

Repeat the breathing exercise for ten minutes, and then open your eyes slowly. Lift your eyes to the skies and thank the lunar energy you have invoked.

> *"Mother Moon, I ask you to keep me safe and join me in my journey; bring your love and feminine energy to my world."*

Take a Moon Bath in the Evening

If you have a bathtub, Monday is the perfect time to run a bath and soak away your woes. Add white sage leaves and Himalayan pink salt to hot water and gently lower yourself into the water. Add a white candle to each corner of the bath and light them safely. Take a piece of paper and a pen with you and write your intentions, dreams, and hopes on the paper. As you relax, visualize the future and what it holds for you.

When you leave the bath, allow yourself to dry as naturally as possible and place your paper beneath a relevant crystal on your altar. Blow out the candles and return to your normal evening routine. Finish the day with a Moon tea made from your favorite herbs and relax into your bed with a soothing energy, ready to sleep.

Set Moon Intentions

Monday is the best time to set intentions, and these can be as varied as you like. Use candles to make your intentions stringer with corresponding colors and list what you want from your love life, your career, and other important aspects of your life. Make this a fun project that can be added to as the week progresses. Use visual images to make more impact and colored pens to make it more artistic.

Don't Be Too Hard on Yourself

Monday's emotions can be brutal, and the lunar energy you feel can take you on a roller coaster ride. Honor and recognize these emotions but don't get upset by them. Your Moon energy is all part of life's great adventure, so get on board and enjoy the ride.

Tuesday

Mars rules this day and brings his passionate, fiery energy to your life. It's time to stop contemplating and start doing. Embrace the fire and brimstone way of life and start to make progress in areas you feel passionate about. Mars will bring you that get-up-and-go energy you need to determine your life path. It may be the traditional second day of the week, but it is the first for energy and domination.

Clothing

Wear your passion with pride and dress in red, maroon, or scarlet tones and look like the warrior you want to become. Wear gemstones like garnets or red coral and celebrate the number nine.

Foods

Prepare a spicy curry in your slow cooker for your evening meal, or plan a tasty takeaway from your favorite restaurant. Tuesday may seem mundane to most people, but you know different. Tuesday is the day of fire and force, so celebrate that fact and have food that ignites your passions.

Meditate in the Morning

Dress your altar with red items and light three red candles. Stand in front of the altar and raise your hands upwards. Take a deep breath and say,

> *"Lord of Mars, I ask you to take my hand and my heart to help me go forward today, make my steps brave and purposeful as I seek my purpose."*

Donate

If you make any donations, make them on a Tuesday. You can give red clothing or copper articles to signal your connection to the benevolent side of Mars's personality. Give your friends and family red hibiscus flowers to show your love and appreciation for them.

Go to the Gym

Make time before your day starts to exercise or go to the gym. Physical exercising will increase your heart rate and push these endorphins to the limit. Get yourself pumped up for the day and tell yourself you will get results.

Join New Organizations

It's time to expand your horizons and seek new contacts. Do they have social groups in your workplace? Ask around as you never know. You may join a group that lets you shine in front of people who normally wouldn't come into contact with you. Chances aren't just given, and sometimes, you must make your own luck.

Complete a Mars Ritual in the Evening

Take a red candle and draw the glyph of Mars on its side. Light an appropriate incense stick like Dragons Blood and light the flame on the candle. Stare into the flame and visualize energy flowing like a molten lava stream into your body. Feel the heat as the energy of Mars fills your veins. When you have completed your ritual, thank the energy of Mars, and open your eyes. Extinguish the candle and thank the universe for your experience.

Take a Ritual Bath

Use sandalwood, mustard seeds, vanilla, and hyssop oil to make a refreshing bath. Place four red candles on each side of the bath and light them. As you bathe, visualize what you'll achieve tomorrow and the next day. Who will recognize your talent, and what will happen when they do?

Now go to bed and dream of what could happen when you work with the power of Mars. Create and change but remember to be victorious.

Wednesday

Mercury is the ruling planet of this pivotal day, and this makes it the perfect time to get your ducks in order. The name of the day originates from Odin, the Old Norse god, so maybe you can take time to say a prayer in his name and offer up a gift on your altar to his wisdom. Odin was also a mischievous god with many human qualities, making Wednesday a day for fun activities and meeting up with friends.

Clothing

To celebrate the energy of Wednesday and Mercury, wear purple or green with splashes of yellow or orange. This sounds like it would clash, but the colors of the day don't have to be your full outfit. Represent them with accessories or jewelry.

Foods

Wednesday is a busy day for planetary energy, so keep your foods light and maybe consider having a day of detox. Clearing out your digestive system will help you focus on more pressing mental issues and prepare you for a day of successful activities. Your body will thank you, and your mind will feel clearer and more focused.

The amount of food containing additives and toxic chemicals is mind-boggling. Never before has there been such a high number of additives and unnatural ingredients included in our food. Perhaps the most disturbing fact is that the companies who make them declare them to be healthy and encourage us to eat them.

Try These Healthy Foods to Stop Toxins

- Lemons are the best detox fruit you can find. Add a few drops to your tea or drink lemon water to boost your metabolism.
- Avocados are natural healers of the liver. The fatty acids and the wealth of nutrients make it a firm favorite for detox.
- Apples contain pectin, which helps cleanse the bloodstream.
- Garlic enhances detoxification and protects the DNA.

Get Organized

Make Wednesday your day to tidy up those emails, get rid of old files on your devices, and make some major decisions. If you keep a manifestation journal, make sure you write in it and be honest with your progress.

Ask Mercury for His Help

Take time before you go to bed to celebrate Mercury by placing citrine and agate on your altar. Light a purple candle and sprinkle some rosemary on your altar.

When you go to bed, close your eyes, and visualize what lies ahead. Success and strong family ties should be strengthened and celebrated.

Thursday

This day of the week is named after one of the most popular Marvel characters and a powerful Norse god, Thor. Thursday's planet is Jupiter, filling the day with masculinity and consecration. It's a day for good luck, prosperity, and cleansing.

Colors

Today you can wear whatever you like. The strength of the energy surrounding you means that even if you were dressed in a trash bag, your personality and self-confidence mean you can carry it off with aplomb.

Deal With Any Legal Matters

Have you been putting stuff off because it is complicated and stressful? Let's embrace a new era of organization that you started on Wednesday and go that extra step and deal with serious matters. If you have legal issues, decide whether you feel confident enough to get it done yourself or whether it is time to call in the professionals.

Change Your Luck

Jupiter is the planet of good luck, and Thursday is the day to test that power. Nobody suggests you start gambling or buy lottery tickets unless you are comfortable with the process, but it is time to remove any bad luck that may affect your life.

Dress your altar in amethysts and turquoise, and sprinkle some cinnamon and garlic on the surface. Light a white candle anointed with your favorite essential oil and say the following phrase:

> *"Mighty Jupiter, remove my hex and make my life a lucky one, bring prosperity and wealth to my home, and bless me with your power."*

Change the Karma

Bad luck could result from negative karma from former lives, so use Thursdays to change that. Do good deeds that are selfless and which attract good karma. Let someone go in line before you and put a dollar bill under five different car windshields. If you see a parking meter that is about to run out, drop a coin in it. Your selfless acts will increase your karmic deposits and help you change your luck.

Practice the Law of Attraction

Choose your favorite meditation pose and shift your perspective. Become more invested in your spiritual growth and let go of negativity. Light a candle and ask Jupiter to bring fortune into your life. Create a vision board in your mind and fill it with photos or images of what you want. Create groups of your dreams. For instance, make a section for your home life, one for your love life, and one for your career. Do you have specific needs or wants? Add them as well.

Of course, you can become more proactive and make a real vision board to represent your wishes physically. Remember to make it as honestly as you can. If you dream of driving a flashy sports car, then represent it on your board. Write your thanks to the universe in the center and place it in the wealth area of your home. If you don't automatically know where this is, stand at your door and walk purposefully to the most south-easterly point of your home.

Friday

This day is named after Freya or Frigg, the Norse goddesses. Even though the two goddesses may claim Friday, they are very similar in personalities and share the same qualities. In planetary terms, Friday is ruled by Venus, and she brings the power of love and passion to the day.

Colors

Wear red and pink with joy and love. Show your happy side and wear your heart on your sleeve. Add silver and white accessories to signal your intention to be filled with love and passion.

Food

Create lavish feasts for people you love. Invite them to your home and celebrate the togetherness you feel when they share your space. If you are passionate about your home, share this energy with others.

Have a Date Night

Putting others before your relationship can become a habit if you are in a relationship or a marriage. You can neglect each other and drift apart. Change that by making Friday date night and getting someone else to look after the kids. Go to a nice restaurant and make a vow to talk about anything except the children, the house, or other day-to-day subjects. Talk about the future and holidays. Make the night a time to rediscover each other and why you fell in love in the first place.

Discover Self-Love

If you are single, you can still tap into the love and passionate energy of Venus. Dress your altar with rose petals and hibiscus flowers and sprinkle lavender. Add moonstone and rose quartz and light red and pink candles. Ask Venus to bring love to your life and find your perfect partner or ask her to bless your single life and fill your heart with love for yourself.

Once you have completed the ritual, it's time to treat yourself to a face mask, a mani-pedi, and a relaxing bath. Add essential oils and light some red candles to create a perfect haven for you to chill and relax.

Watch a Romantic Film

Although Friday is traditionally a night to socialize, get yourself in the mood for love by watching a romantic film. This doesn't have to be a traditional love story as there are plenty of films that deal with all sorts of love. Marley and Me, a film starring Owen Wilson and Jennifer Aniston, is about family and the love they share with their children, themselves, and a favorite family pet. BE aware that you'll need a tissue at some point!

Attract Love

Do you have a crush? Try to attract their attention by casting a love spell by writing their name on a piece of paper and placing it beneath a red candle on your altar. Ask Venus to let this person know you are interested and then sit back and wait. If it is meant to be, they will be in touch soon.

Get Physical

If it has been a while since you were intimate with your partner, make Friday the night of love. Be sexy and dress in your finest nightwear or leave the clothes off to send signals to your other half. Be adventurous and make time for sex and romance. Bathe together or take a quick shower to get your juices flowing. Don't hold back, but remember those early feelings when you just couldn't get enough of each other. Try and recreate those passions, and you could be in for a night filled with hot and steamy action.

Saturday

Ruled by Saturn, this is a day to get motivated and become proactive. However, it is also a day for relaxing. Divide your day into different sections and use the early part of the day to clear up any work that is still outstanding from the week before. Prepare the meals for the week ahead on paper or physically to make sure you know that mealtimes are covered.

Plan Ahead

With your meal plan in place, it is now time to organize yourself and any other people who have plans for the week ahead. Do the kids have sports or social engagements? Make sure any kit or clothing they need is washed and stacked, ready to add to their bags. Do you have meetings or presentations at work? Check that you have appropriate clothing in your wardrobe that is ready to wear and matched to relevant accessories.

Have a Power Breakfast

Saturn encompasses energy so prepare your body for an active day. Eat oats and berries to give you long-lasting energy and help digestion. Avocado on toast will keep you full until lunch and provide antioxidants. Yogurt and blueberries are super tasty and packed with calcium and protein, while kale and goat cheese are low in calories and packed with protein.

Perform a Saturn Ritual

Saturday is the perfect time to create a safe zone for your spiritual energy. It isn't as confronting as the energy of Mars. It simply takes any heat out of spiritual bullets coming your way.

Decorate your altar with yellow and black candles, and add onyx and jet to the surface. Draw the glyph of Saturn and add the letters H and T to represent heart and truth. Use peppermint oil to anoint the candles and add moss to the altar. Ask Saturn to protect you from spiritual attacks and keep you safe and strong. Ask for his help to locate things or people you may have lost or misplaced. Liberate your energy and begin some self-transformation by channeling the energy of Saturn.

Sunday

The day of the Sun and all his rejuvenating powers. Most people experience anxiety on Sunday, especially in school. That dreadful feeling that you have forgotten something or haven't done your homework, your gym kit isn't ready, or you have lost part of the uniform. Unfortunately, we carry that level of anxiety with us into adult life.

Colors

Reflect the solar system's energy by wearing bright colors and clothes that make you feel happy. Be relaxed and happy in your comfortable clothes but remember to reflect your happiness onto others. Wear your favorite jewelry and accessories to show you have made an effort.

Relax and Unwind

While you have your breakfast, play relaxing and inspiring music. Create a Sunday playlist with your favorite tunes and play them while you get ready for your day. Eat slowly and mindfully as you let the sounds wash over you and help you to feel chilled.

Celebrate the Sun

Take the rest of the day to set intentions, heal yourself and embrace the power of abundance. Turn your face to the sky and feel the sun's rays fill you with hope and love. Decorate your altar with sunflowers, marigolds, and citrine crystals. Burn orange and yellow candles and thank the Sun for its presence in your life every day.

Prepare Yourself for the Week Ahead

This is possibly the most important part of your week. Some people will prepare their bodies with exercise, while some will meditate or read a good book to prepare the mind. This is your time for a routine and your inner energies. Whatever suits you should dictate what you do. Walking in nature may work for some while others may prefer a night with friends.

This guide is an interchangeable set of activities and rituals that can be adapted to suit the day's energy. Planetary magick is all about connecting with the universe and becoming part of the bigger picture.

Conclusion

Now you have your comprehensive guide to the planets, it's time to connect and explore. We are all part of the cosmos, and we should intentionally celebrate this fact! Be kinder to yourself and others and change how you view the universe. We all benefit from kindness and connectivity, so be a catalyst for change. Good luck with your journey, and *spread the love.*

Here's another book by Mari Silva that you might like

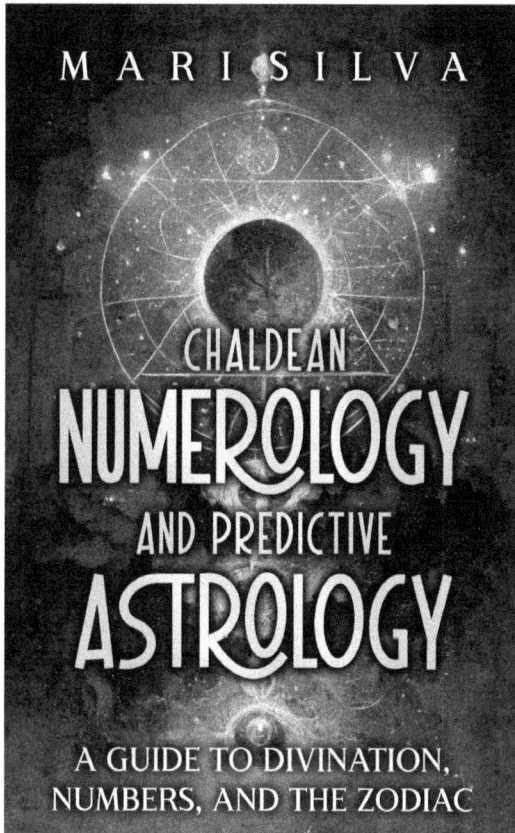

MARI SILVA

CHALDEAN
NUMEROLOGY
AND PREDICTIVE
ASTROLOGY

A GUIDE TO DIVINATION,
NUMBERS, AND THE ZODIAC

Your Free Gift
(only available for a limited time)

Thanks for getting this book! If you want to learn more about various spirituality topics, then join Mari Silva's community and get a free guided meditation MP3 for awakening your third eye. This guided meditation mp3 is designed to open and strengthen ones third eye so you can experience a higher state of consciousness. Simply visit the link below the image to get started.

https://spiritualityspot.com/meditation

Resources

5 Minor Dwarf Planets In Astrology & Their Meanings. (2021, February 25). YourTango. https://www.yourtango.com/2021339761/dwarf-minor-planets-meanings-astrology#:~:text=Makemake%20symbolizes%20a%20connection%20to

12 Astrology Zodiac Signs Dates, Meanings, and Compatibility. (2000). Astrology-Zodiac-Signs.com. https://www.astrology-zodiac-signs.com/

12 Zodiac Signs: All You Need to Know | Astrology.com. (n.d.). Www.astrology.com. https://www.astrology.com/zodiac-signs

A Brief History of Astrology. (2020). Astrograph.com. https://www.astrograph.com/learning-astrology/history.php

An Introduction to Secondary Progressions | Kepler Astrological Education. (n.d.). Www.keplercollege.org. from https://www.keplercollege.org/index.php/articles-opinions/using-astrology/1010-into-secondary-prog

Archive, V. A., & feed, G. author R. (2021, November 16). What is a birth chart in astrology — and how do you read one? New York Post. https://nypost.com/article/astrology-birth-chart/

Asteroids in Astrology and Their Meaning | Astrology.com. (n.d.). www.astrology.com . from https://www.astrology.com/asteroids

Astrology Planets and their Meanings, Planet Symbols and Cheat Sheet. (2018, January 27). Labyrinthos. https://labyrinthos.co/blogs/astrology-horoscope-zodiac-signs/astrology-planets-and-their-meanings-planet-symbols-and-cheat-sheet

Beringer-Tobing, B. (2021, October 7). Here's How Aspects in Your Birth Chart Play a Large Role in Your Day-to-Day Life. POPSUGAR Smart Living.

https://www.popsugar.com/smart-living/what-aspects-mean-in-astrology-48534359#:~:text=Simply%20put%2C%20aspects%20refer%20to

Beringer-Tobing, B. (2022, April 8). Every Major Asteroid in Astrology, Explained. POPSUGAR Smart Living. https://www.popsugar.com/smart-living/asteroids-astrology-48779069#:~:text=Asteroids%20can%20tell%20you%20a

Besley, T. (2017, January 17). How to make astrology a regular practice in your life. The Little Red Tarot Blog. http://blog.littleredtarot.com/make-astrology-regular-practice/

Brennan, C. (2007, October 19). 10 Tips For Learning Astrology. The Horoscopic Astrology Blog. http://horoscopicastrologyblog.com/2007/10/19/10-tips-for-learning-astrology/

Brown, M. (2021, August 11). What Is Astrology, Actually? InStyle. https://www.instyle.com/lifestyle/astrology/what-is-astrology

Campos, S. N. (n.d.-a). Forget Your Sun Sign: Your Node Pairing Sheds Light on Your Life Path | Astrology.com. Www.astrology.com. from https://www.astrology.com/article/nodes-north-south-pairings-destiny-zodiac/

Campos, S. N. (n.d.-b). Your North and South Nodes Hold the Keys to Your Karma | Astrology.com. Www.astrology.com. from https://www.astrology.com/article/nodes-north-south-moon-karma-destiny/

Coughlin, S. (2017, December 4). Those Mysterious Astrological Symbols, Explained. Www.refinery29.com. https://www.refinery29.com/en-us/zodiac-astrology-symbols-meanings#slide-1

Coughlin, S. (2018a, June 1). What It Actually Means When Your Horoscope Mentions A "Transit." Www.refinery29.com. https://www.refinery29.com/en-us/transit-astrology-meaning-natal-planets

Coughlin, S. (2018b, September 20). This Astrological Chart Shows How Your Personality Changes Over Time. Www.refinery29.com. https://www.refinery29.com/en-us/progressed-birth-chart-astrology-meaning

Coughlin, S. (2022, May 3). How To Make Sense Of Your Birth Chart. Www.refinery29.com. https://www.refinery29.com/en-us/2016/11/129929/birth-chart-analysis-natal-astrology-reading

Crystals and Astrology; What Do They Have in Common? (2020, May 14). Happinez.com. https://www.happinez.com/blog/crystals-and-astrology/

Dawn, C. (2021, April 18). Foundations of Astrology- As Above, So Below. Moonstone Lightworks. https://www.moonstonelightworks.com/post/foundations-of-astrology-as-above-so-below

---

DeSimone, M. (2021, November 29). The Significance of Progressed Birth Charts in Astrology. Tarot.com. https://www.tarot.com/astrology/birth-chart-progressions

Ephemeris. (n.d.). A Brief History of Astrology. Ephemeris. https://ephemeris.co/pages/a-brief-history-of-astrology

Faragher, A. K. (2021, June 8). What Each "House" Represents in Your Birth Chart. Allure. https://www.allure.com/story/12-astrology-houses-meaning

Hall, M. (2018, April 30). Understand the Basics of Astrology. LiveAbout. https://www.liveabout.com/what-is-astrology-206723

HISTORY OF ASTROLOGY. (2019). Historyworld.net. http://www.historyworld.net/wrldhis/PlainTextHistories.asp?historyid=ac32

History of Western Astrology. (n.d.). TheFreeDictionary.com. https://encyclopedia2.thefreedictionary.com/History+of+Western+Astrology

How To Interpret North Nodes & South Nodes To Find Your True Purpose. (2020, December 28). Mindbodygreen. https://www.mindbodygreen.com/articles/astrology-101-north-nodes-south-nodes-reveal-your-life-purpose/

How to interpret your Birth Chart. (n.d.). Tree of Life. https://treeoflife.com.au/blogs/news/how-to-interpret-your-birth-chart#:~:text=A%20Birth%20Chart%20is%20what

How To Read Secondary Progressions. (n.d.). Two Wander. https://www.twowander.com/blog/how-to-read-secondary-progressions

How To Read Your Birth Chart Like An Astrologer. (2019, January 31). Mindbodygreen. https://www.mindbodygreen.com/articles/how-to-read-your-astrology-birth-chart/

Jan. 2, J. W. |, & 2022. (2022, January 2). The 12 Houses of Astrology, Explained. PureWow. https://www.purewow.com/wellness/12-houses-of-astrology

June, S. (2021, September 21). Black Moon Lilith In Astrology, Explained. Nylon. https://www.nylon.com/life/black-moon-lilith-astrology

Kahn, N. (2018, October 17). What Do North Nodes & South Nodes Mean In Astrology? They Show You How To Embrace Your Destiny. Bustle. https://www.bustle.com/p/what-do-north-nodes-south-nodes-mean-in-astrology-they-show-you-how-to-embrace-your-destiny-12577188

Kathryn. (2021, February 19). Astrology Transits - What are they, and how can you work with them? Kathryn Hocking. https://kathrynhocking.com/transits-in-astrology/

Lantz, P. (n.d.). Astrological Progression for Beginners. LoveToKnow. https://horoscopes.lovetoknow.com/about-astrology/astrological-progression-beginners

Learn Astrology: 10 Tips for Beginners. (2021, September 26). MIND IS the MASTER. https://mindisthemaster.com/learn-astrology/

Major and Minor Aspects. (n.d.). Home. https://astrologyinaction.com/major-and-minor-aspects

Major Planetary Aspect Meanings - Relationship Between Planets in Astrology, Zodiac Signs and Natal Charts. (n.d.). Labyrinthos. https://labyrinthos.co/blogs/astrology-horoscope-zodiac-signs/planetary-aspect-meanings-relationship-between-planets-in-astrology-zodiac-signs-and-natal-charts

Massony, T. (2022, January 5). Here's When to Expect Every Planet's Retrograde Periods in 2022. POPSUGAR Smart Living. https://www.popsugar.com/smart-living/what-planets-are-retrograde-right-now-48669539

Minor Aspects in Astrology: Quincunx, Semisquare, Semi-Sextile, Quintile. (2021, August 13). Advanced Astrology. https://advanced-astrology.com/minor-aspects/

Minor astrological aspects and the domain of magic. (2019, May 30). Time Nomad. https://timenomad.app/posts/astrology/philosophy/2019/05/30/minor-aspects-domain-of-magic.html#:~:text=Minor%20astrological%20aspects%20are%20responsible

Odyssey, D. (n.d.). Asteroids In Astrology & Their Meanings, Explained. Nylon. https://www.nylon.com/life/asteroids-astrology-meaning

Orion, R. (2021, August 10). How to Identify Overall Patterns on Your Astrological Birth Chart. Dummies. https://www.dummies.com/article/body-mind-spirit/religion-spirituality/astrology/how-to-identify-overall-patterns-on-your-astrological-birth-chart-268214/

Pholus - The Power of Small Actions Leading to Great Awakenings. (n.d.). 12andUs. https://12andus.com/blog/view/396023/pholus-the-power-of-small-actions-leading-to-great-awakenings

Planetary Colors and Gemstones. (n.d.). Jupiters

Regan, S. (2022, April 19). The Most & Least Lucky Aspects To Have On Your Zodiac Chart, From Astrologers. Mindbodygreen. https://www.mindbodygreen.com/articles/aspects-in-astrology

Robinson, K. (n.d.). North Node in Astrology: Meaning, Signs, Symbol North Node in Astrology: Meaning, Signs, Symbol | Astrology.com. www.astrology.com. https://www.astrology.com/article/north-node-meaning/

Rudhyar, D. (n.d.). Understanding the Basics of Astrology | Basic Astrology for Beginners. Dawn Mountain. http://www.dawnmountain.com/understanding-the-basics-of-astrology/

Secondary Progressions. (n.d.). Astrolibrary.org. https://astrolibrary.org/category/progressions/

Secondary Progressions | Cafe Astrology .com. (n.d.). Cafeastrology.com. https://cafeastrology.com/secondaryprogressions.html

Secondary Progressions: More | Cafe Astrology .com. (n.d.). Cafeastrology.com. https://cafeastrology.com/astrologyofprogressions.html

Sloan, E. (2021, July 13). Here's What Each Planet Actually Means in Astrology—So You Can Understand Your Chart in More Depth. Well+Good. https://www.wellandgood.com/meanings-of-planets-in-astrology/

Solar Arc Directions. (n.d.). Astrology School. https://astrologyschool.net/solar-arc-directions/

"As Above, so Below": Meaning & Interpretation. 6 Dec. 2020, https://linguaholic.com/linguablog/as-above-so-below-meaning/?msclkid=a8f1b824c38311ecad5294ca460c6463

"5 Venus Rituals to Invoke the Divine Feminine." Oui We, www.ouiwegirl.com/beauty/2020/10/10/5-venus-rituals-to-invoke-the-divine-feminine

"10 Best Guided Meditation Scripts | Jupiter." Getjupiter.com, 25 Jan. 2022, https://getjupiter.com/blogs/wellness/free-guided-meditation-scripts

Administrator, Author Site. "The Planetary Deities." Green Planet Astrology, 30 Dec. 2016, https://greenplanetastrology.wordpress.com/2016/12/30/the-planetary-deities/?msclkid=50295b89c6aa11ecbc701363bcdd906a

Arcane, Arcane. "Picatrix." Grimoire Magic, 2 Sept. 2020, https://booksofmagick.com/picatrix/?msclkid=cee86f71c38511ecb387a709b95a38e2

astrologerbydefault. "Planets Energies and Food You Love." Psychologically Astrology, 15 Jan. 2019, https://psychologicallyastrology.com/2019/01/15/planetary-energies-of-the-food-you-love/#:~:text=Plants%20naturally%20produce%20such%20chemicals%20in%20minute%20quantities

Avia. "God Symbols Mars." What's-Your-Sign.com, 7 Feb. 2018, www.whats-your-sign.com/god-symbols-mars.html?msclkid=f3305d69c83711ec9b277908c184c3a9

"Correspondences of Mercury and Its Earth and Air Aspects from Alchemy Works." Www.alchemy-Works.com, www.alchemy-works.com/planets_mercury.html?msclkid=d8ceee1cc79111ec953f5903f8879326

"Each Day Has a Planet That Goes with It — Here's How You Can Harness This Energy." Elite Daily, www.elitedaily.com/lifestyle/what-planet-rules-each-day

"EFFECTIVE LOVE SPELLS through GODDESS VENUS." Love Spells, 4 June 2020, https://lovespell.tips/effective-love-spells-through-goddess-venus/

"Effects of Jupiter Benefic or Malefic in Horoscope - Astrology." Vedic Astrology & Ayurveda, 18 Sept. 2014, www.astrogle.com/astrology/effects-jupiter-benefic-malefic-horoscope.html

Enhance Your Money Spells with Jupiter Energy - Black Witch Coven. 22 Mar. 2017, https://blackwitchcoven.com/enhance-your-money-spells-with-jupiter-energy/

happy.com.pt, Happy. "Jupiter in Astrology - Meaning, Signs and Birth Chart • AstroMundus." AstroMundus, 25 Apr. 2021, https://astromundus.com/en/jupiter-astrology/

---. "Mars in Astrology - Meaning, Signs and Birth Chart • AstroMundus." AstroMundus, 25 Apr. 2021, https://astromundus.com/en/mars-astrology/?msclkid=48d3f725c83711ecb27e48ee8a7b4947

---. "Mercury in Astrology - Meaning, Signs and Birth Chart • AstroMundus." AstroMundus, 26 Apr. 2021, https://astromundus.com/en/mercury-astrology?msclkid=2498a75ec76f11ecb494b5f0c62ef741

---. "Saturn in Astrology - Meaning, Signs and Birth Chart • AstroMundus." AstroMundus, 26 Apr. 2021, https://astromundus.com/en/saturn-astrology/

---. "The Moon in Astrology - Meaning, Signs and Birth Chart • AstroMundus." AstroMundus, 26 Apr. 2021, https://astromundus.com/en/moon-astrology/?msclkid=c205ac48c6a911ec8b3c6dfb5127889f.

"How to Create a Sacred Altar for Meditation, Magic & Ritual | She Rose." She Rose Revolution, 10 June 2020, https://revoloon.com/shanijay/062020-how-to-create-a-sacred-altar

"Jupiter." Gods and Goddesses, https://godsandgoddesses.org/roman/jupiter/

"Jupiter - the Planets - the White Goddess." http://www.thewhitegoddess.co.uk/, www.thewhitegoddess.co.uk/the_elements/the_planets/jupiter.asp

Kedia, Surabhi. "Spirit Animal List | a Complete Spirit Animal List and Meanings." TheMindFool - Perfect Medium for Self-Development & Mental Health. Explorer of Lifestyle Choices & Seeker of the Spiritual Journey, 22 Mar. 2020, https://themindfool.com/spirit-animal-list/

ladyoftheabyss. "Full Moon Colours, Herbs, Oils, Incense and Much More." Witches of the Craft®, 1 July 2015, https://witchesofthecraft.com/2015/07/01/full-moon-colours-herbs-oils-incense-and-much-more/?msclkid=6dad3f44c6ab11ec8500c6c8e727e8c7

"List of Solar Deities." Religion Wiki, https://religion.fandom.com/wiki/List_of_solar_deities?msclkid=0d23ada3c51411ec9047b0bb68c4f708

"Lunar Spirit Animal Symbolism and Meaning - Moon Animal Symbolism." ZodiacSigns-Horoscope.com, 24 May 2019, www.zodiacsigns-horoscope.com/spirit-animals/lunar-spirit-animal-symbolism/?msclkid=94559fa9c6aa11ecacb674a2145041f7

"Magical Days of the Week: Correspondences & Daily Energy." Otherworldly Oracle, 22 Apr. 2020, https://otherworldlyoracle.com/magical-days-of-the-week/

"Mars - the Planets - the White Goddess." Www.thewhitegoddess.co.uk, www.thewhitegoddess.co.uk/the_elements/the_planets/mars.asp?msclkid=4c4f4577c83811eca99c32b508dcd16d

Meaning of Jupiter in Astrology: The Greater Benefic - Astrology. advanced-

"Mercury." Gods and Demons Wiki,

moodymoons. "Sun Magic and Witchcraft." Moody Moons, 7 Apr. 2015, https://www.moodymoons.com/2015/04/07/sun-magick/?msclkid=3edecbdfc51411ec86775090d9626a86.

Penczak, Christopher. "Planetary Magic 5: Mars and Victory." Christopher Penczak, 29 July 2013, https://christopherpenczak.com/2013/07/29/planetary-magic-5-mars-and-victory/

"Personality Traits That Moon Sign Charts Reveal." Astrology Bay, 11 Jan. 2008, https://astrologybay.com/moon-sign-charts?msclkid=1bf8d615c6aa11ec9080a15acd122a75.

PowerofPositivity. "5 Things Reading Your Birth Chart Will Teach You." Power of Positivity: Positive Thinking & Attitude, 13 Aug. 2015, www.powerofpositivity.com/5-things-reading-your-birth-chart-will-teach-you/#:~:text=Your%20birth%20chart%20will%20show%20you%20that%20you

"Role and Importance of Planets in Astrology." Shrivinayakaastrology.com, https://shrivinayakaastrology.com/Planets/roleofplanets.html?msclkid=75a3b965c48111ec8424ee272b586e4d.

"Saturn - the Planets - the White Goddess." Www.thewhitegoddess.co.uk, www.thewhitegoddess.co.uk/the_elements/the_planets/saturn.asp

Secrets of the Magickal Grimoires: The Classical Texts of Magick Deciphered – Aaron Leitch – OCCULT WORLD. https://occult-world.com/secrets-of-the-magickal-grimoires/

"Solar Animal Symbolism." Sun Signs, 26 July 2016, www.sunsigns.org/solar-animal-symbolism/#:~:text=Two%20other%20creatures%2C%20the%20rooster%20and%20the%20dragon%2C

"Solar Witch: How to Cast SUN MAGICK in 11 Ways." Otherworldly Oracle, 30 Aug. 2020, https://otherworldlyoracle.com/solar-witch/?msclkid=c0061049c51211ec9a05292bedcb236a

"Sun in Astrology |." Astroligion.com, 26 Sept. 2020, https://astroligion.com/sun-in-astrology/?msclkid=b4b0060ac54411ecb6e2b4dc1ea7b7c1

"The Essential Dignities of Planets: Exalted, Detriment, Domicile, and Fall | the AstroTwins." Astrostyle: Astrology and Daily, Weekly, Monthly Horoscopes by the AstroTwins, 15 Aug. 2020, https://astrostyle.com/astrology/essential-dignities/?msclkid=bced7594c45611ecb3766a96d43aa31f

"The Ultimate Full Moon Ritual for Beginners." Soul Design by Sarah Kreuz, www.sarahkreuz.co/moon-rituals/full-moon-rituals-for-beginners?msclkid=6cc51403c6cf11ec961da1d207da5984

"What Are Spiritual Altars & How Can You Make One? | Astrology Answers." AstrologyAnswers.com, https://www.astrologyanswers.com/article/what-are-spiritual-altars-how-can-you-make-one/

"What Is an Astrology Birth Chart? Your Natal Chart Explained." Astrostyle: Astrology and Daily, Weekly, Monthly Horoscopes by the AstroTwins, https://astrostyle.com/astrology/birth-chart/?msclkid=6471399ec45511ec80a07c7c0a404e8b.

"What Is Planetary Magic?" Arnemancy, 27 July 2020, https://arnemancy.com/articles/practice/what-is-planetary-magic/?msclkid=93f3e5ecc38611ec89e26c7b3faa4e33.

Witchipedian, The. "Venus." The Witchipedia, 9 July 2019, https://witchipedia.com/astrology/venus/

"Working with the Powerful Mercury Energy (Witchcraft Tips)." Magickalspot.com, 8 Sept. 2021, https://magickalspot.com/mercury-energy/#:~:text=The%20best%20day%20for%20you%20to%20work%20with.